Innovation und Entrepreneurship

Innovative Konzepte und unternehmerische Leistungen sind für Wohlstand und Fortschritt von entscheidender Bedeutung. Diese Schriftenreihe vereint wissenschaftliche Arbeiten zu diesem Themenbereich. Sie beschreiben substanzielle Erkenntnisse auf hohem methodischen Niveau.

Alexander Hoffmann

Value Capture in Disintegrated Value Chains

The Hierarchy Strategy

With a Foreword by Prof. Dr. Joachim Henkel

Springer Gabler

Alexander Hoffmann
Munich, Germany

Dissertation TU Munich, 2015

Innovation und Entrepreneurship
ISBN 978-3-658-11367-4 ISBN 978-3-658-11368-1 (eBook)
DOI 10.1007/978-3-658-11368-1

Library of Congress Control Number: 2015955142

Springer Gabler

Printed on acid-free paper

Springer Gabler is a brand of Springer Fachmedien Wiesbaden
Springer Fachmedien Wiesbaden is part of Springer Science+Business Media
(www.springer.com)

Foreword

Among the numerous questions that occupy management practitioners and scholars, one question is arguably central: What is it that makes a firm profitable? Researchers have identified a broad range of factors, in particular a firm's resources and its market environment. Related to a firm's environment, the concept of "industry architecture" proved helpful in further understanding the differential profitability of firms. However, this concept has an important gap: it does not account for the position that a firm occupies in the various value chains that it is part of. Yet, a firm might supply the same input for the same final product as a tier-one or a tier-two supplier. Surely, this position should affect its profitability.

This is where Alexander Hoffmann's dissertation makes an important contribution. The author shows, using sophisticated game-theoretical models, how a firm's position in the value chain – everything else equal – should affect the share of the overall industry profit that it can capture. Using powerful and well-researched case studies Alexander Hoffmann then demonstrates empirically that a firm may indeed find itself on various levels of the value chain even though its own contribution remains unchanged.

This dissertation is the result of intense and dedicated research, requiring analytical skills as well as creativity and commitment. It was a pleasure to be part of this endeavor as Alexander Hoffmann's dissertation advisor. The concepts and results developed in this work provide important insights to research and practice, and I recommend it to scholars and practitioners alike.

Joachim Henkel

Munich, July 21, 2015

Acknowledgements

I am indebted to many people for their support and encouragement and want to take this opportunity to warmly thank all of you who contributed to the success of my thesis.

First, let me express my deepest gratitude to my scientific advisor, Prof. Dr. Joachim Henkel. I am deeply grateful for your continuous support, valuable advice, and honest feedback. Thank you for the great learning experience throughout which you generously shared your time in many interesting discussions and problem-solving sessions. I am also grateful to Prof. Dr. Martin Grunow for reviewing my dissertation and to Prof. Dr. Christoph Kaserer for chairing my dissertation committee.

The empirical section of this research work was made possible through the generous support of industry experts who shared their time, valuable insights, and thoughts. In particular, I thank Harald Jungerberg, who used his contacts to find practitioners to participate in interviews that enabled me to gain a full understanding of the laundry dryer value chain.

Further, I thank and recognize my colleagues, Rainer Filitz, Markus Hagenmaier, Dominik Hepp, Robert Lüttke, Philipp Pfingstag, Stephanie Preißner. Christina Raasch, Anja Schön, Tim Schweisfurth, Katharina Tanimura, Evelin Winands, Michael Zaggl, and Hans Zischka for creating a great atmosphere and fun working environment at the Dr. Theo Schöller Chair in Technology and Innovation Management.

I am deeply indebted to my parents and my brother for their encouragement and unconditional support. Thank you for being there for me.

My deepest and most sincere gratitude to my wonderful wife, Alice, and my son, Maximilian, for continuous support throughout my academic work and beyond. You bring so much joy into my life. This thesis is dedicated to you!

Alexander Hoffmann

Munich, January 2015

Table of Contents

List of Appendices

List of Figures

List of Tables

List of Abbreviations

BSH	Bosch Siemens Hausgeräte GmbH
E.G.O.	E.G.O. Blanc und Fischer & Co. GmbH
HC	Hierarchical Core
HSV	Hierarchical Shapley value
L1	Top-level or level one of a hierarchical bargaining structure
L2	Level two of a hierarchical bargaining structure
LTE	Long Term Evolution
NVA	Non-value-appropriating
OEM	Original equipment manufacturer
OV	Owen value
SV	Shapley value

Abstract

Today, value chains design and produce most goods and the value captured as a whole is distributed among the chain's members through bargaining. For complex products bargaining typically comprises several individual negotiations structured according to the hierarchical organization of the respective industry. In this research, I introduce the notion of "bargaining structure" to describe the sequence and participants of these individual negotiations.

Using cooperative game theory—in particular the Shapley value and extensions of it—I show how bargaining structure affects the distribution of value among the constituent firms of the value chain. I find that positions in the bargaining structure most conducive to value capture are those where large complementarity gains are realized and split, ideally, among a small number of negotiators.

Since the bargaining structure of a value chain is to some extent malleable, each member has an incentive to shape it in such a way as to optimize its own value capture. I suggest that the bargaining structure is shaped by the underlying architecture of the value chain and the action of powerful firms. Product architecture is a key lever to influence the architecture of the value chain and can be used to shape bargaining structure and enhance value capture. Using examples from the commercial aircraft and the white goods industries, the results of my research posit that bargaining structures are indeed malleable and, to some extent, under the control of the central firm.

Zusammenfassung

Eine Vielzahl von Gütern wird heute durch Beiträge verschiedener Unternehmen entwickelt und produziert. Der Wert, den die Wertschöpfungskette als Ganzes schöpft, wird durch Verhandlungen auf die beitragenden Unternehmen verteilt. Für komplexe Produkte finden typischerweise mehrere einzelnen Verhandlungen statt, die in einer hierarchischen Struktur angeordnet sind. Der Begriff „Verhandlungsstruktur“ umschreibt die Abfolge und Teilnehmer der einzelnen Verhandlungen.

Die vorliegende Dissertation untersucht den Einfluss von Verhandlungsstrukturen auf die Wertaneignung von Unternehmen. Basierend auf kooperativer Spieltheorie, insbesondere dem Shapley-Wert, zeigt diese Arbeit, dass vorteilhafte Positionen in der Verhandlungsstruktur solche sind, in denen große Komplementaritäten erzielt werden, die idealerweise unter einer kleinen Gruppe von verhandelnden Unternehmen aufgeteilt werden.

Da Verhandlungsstrukturen beeinflussbar sind, haben Unternehmen einen Anreiz diese so zu formen, dass sie ihre eigene Wertaneignung maximieren. Zum einen ist die zu Grunde liegende Wertschöpfungskette ein wichtiger Bestimmungsfaktor der Verhandlungsstruktur. Da die Produktarchitektur die Architektur der Wertschöpfungskette mitbestimmt, können Unternehmen über das Produkt die Verhandlungsstruktur und Wertaneignung beeinflussen. Zum anderen können starke Unternehmen mit starker Verhandlungsposition die Verhandlungsstruktur direkt verändern. Beispiele aus dem kommerziellen Flugzeugbau und der Haushaltsgeräteindustrie zeigen, dass Verhandlungsstrukturen in der Tat veränderbar und zu einem Teil unter der Kontrolle eines zentralen Unternehmens sind.

1 Introduction

Discovering what determines a firm's performance in an industry is a core endeavor of business research. While value is jointly created by a chain of firms that contribute to the production of a good or the provision of a service, it may be unevenly distributed among the participating firms. Scholars have approached the determinants of value capture from two different perspectives. While the resource-based view emphasizes ownership and control of critical resources as key to disproportional value capture (Barney 1986; Daft 1983), the market-based view focuses on the structural characteristics of the industry (Bain 1956; Porter 1980). Both streams suggest that attaining a "bottleneck" position by making the firm the most difficult to replace in an industry or value chain, is favorable for value capture (Baldwin 2014; Iansiti and Levien 2004; Jacobides and MacDuffie 2013; Jacobides et al. 2006; Morris and Ferguson 1993; Pisano and Teece 2007; Teece 1986).

Generally, value is split among firms through bargaining (Brandenburger and Stuart 2007). A given firm bargains upstream with its suppliers and downstream with its customers to determine its input and sales prices. A bottleneck position leads to high bargaining power in negotiations, which, in turn, drives value capture.

I define a value chain following Sturgeon (2001) as the collectivity of all firms that contribute to a particular instance of value creation. An industry may comprise several value chains. The distribution of value among value chains in an industry is determined by customers' purchase decisions for core and complementary products. Although this division drives the value available to firms in a specific value chain, I focus solely on the distribution within a value chain.

The literature discusses various approaches to attaining a bottleneck position. Some imply changes to value chain or industry architecture, that is, to the template circumscribing the division of labor among firms (Jacobides et al. 2006). Firms can aim to influence industry architecture either through fostering competition in other segments of the value chain or by reducing competition in its own segment. For example, open interfaces facilitate the development of complementary products, thus, stimulating competition in adjacent parts of the value chain (Eisenmann et al. 2009). Further, firms work to control critical assets tightly, for example, through legal protection mechanisms such as patents (Pisano and Teece 2007), hence, impeding direct competition.

Existing studies have enhanced our understanding of how industry architecture affects value capture through the intensity of competition in various segments of a value chain. Yet, more fundamental variations in the architecture of the industry or value chains are ubiquitous, and their effects are largely unexplored.

As an example, there have been significant structural shifts in the value chain for large, commercial aircrafts. Airbus and Boeing used to be the integrators of a large number of components, however, for the most recent programs of the A350 and the B787 Dreamliner they have handed over responsibility for large sections of the aircraft to selected suppliers. These so-called mega suppliers not only design and integrate the awarded sections but also manage the value chain for the respective system. Concomitantly, firms that used to deal directly with the original equipment manufacturer (OEM) were moved to a lower tier, and now negotiate with and supplying to the integrator of a section. B/E Aerospace, for instance, which supplies oxygen systems, dealt with Airbus directly for earlier programs. However, for the A350, the company supplies these systems to Spirit AeroSystems. Importantly, B/E Aerospace also conducts all related price negotiations with Spirit AeroSystems rather than with Airbus. While implications of the shifts in aircraft value chains on replaceability have been discussed in, for example, Elahi et al. (2014), Pritchard and MacPherson (2004), and Shih and Pierson (2012), the effect of the structural shifts on value capture is unknown.

Such changes to value chains, implying that its members are rearranged, are not considered in the existing literature. In fact, the meaning of "architecture" as describing the structure of the value chain and the linkages among its constituent firms is, so far, largely unexplored. The study by Erat et al. (2013) is a notable exception; however, rather than focus on effects of the structure of negotiations, it explores competitive differentiation and the benefits of outsourcing the integration function.

The present study[1] addresses this gap. Focusing on the value chain as the unit of analysis, I argue that the division of value between its member firms takes place in a hierarchy of negotiations. Typically, the manufacturer of a final good will negotiate with its tier-one suppliers, which, in turn, will negotiate with their respective suppliers. I use

1 Note that this dissertation is the basis for an article that is planned to be published in 2015. Thus, some parts of the documents overlap. A working draft of the paper is published as Henkel and Hoffmann (2014).

the term *bargaining structure* to describe the members of a value chain that negotiate among each other in its various stages and branches, and how these individual negotiation processes are linked hierarchically.[2] The present work analyzes how the bargaining structure of the value chain for a specific product affects the distribution of value among the contributing firms, what factors determine the bargaining structure, and how firms can use this information to enhance value capture.

Using cooperative game theory, I show how bargaining structure influences value distribution. I extend the Shapley value solution concept (Shapley 1953) by introducing the concept of the "hierarchical Shapley value." This concept is used to study the effects of the bargaining structure, essentiality of firms, the role of integrators, and the availability of freely available building blocks (e.g., open source software) on the value split.

A simple example using three firms shows how bargaining structure affects value distribution. There are two possible bargaining structures. Either all three firms bargain jointly on the same level or one firm splits the available value with a representative of the other two firms that subsequently negotiate to split the value captured by their representative. If all firms are essential (in the sense that each firm's absence would reduce the overall value to zero) they would, according to the Shapley value (and to intuition), split the value equally, thus, each obtaining one third if bargaining on one level. However, if the bargaining structure is hierarchical, there are two equal players in the first negotiation sharing the available value equally. While this outcome may appear counterintuitive at first, consider that in the top-level negotiation, the representative is just as essential as the single firm. In the second step, the two firms on the lower level of the bargaining structure would again arrive at an equal split of the value obtained by the representative given that both are essential, each obtaining one quarter. Thus, in this case, a hierarchical bargaining structure dramatically favors the single firm, which secures half rather than one third of the overall value.

A practical implication can be found in the context of patent royalties. Quies (2012) observed that the number of patents owned by a firm that are declared as essential for

---

2 Hierarchy, here, does not imply any ranking in the sense of command-and-execution. Further, firms may participate in various stages of the value chain, thus creating transaction cycles (Luo et al. 2012) and bargaining cycles. For a specific end product, however, the assumption of a hierarchical, tree-like bargaining structure will, in most cases, be fulfilled.

the Long-Term Evolution (LTE) standard, is not necessarily reflected in the announced royalty rates.[3] For example, while Huawei, owning more than 180 essential LTE patents, announced an overall licensing fee of 1.5% of the sales price of handsets, Motorola, owning a far smaller portfolio of 16 essential patents, announced a licensing fee of 2.3%. Hence, a hierarchical bargaining structure in which essential patents are consolidated for negotiations may be disadvantageous for the owners of these patents.

Given that the bargaining structure affects the distribution of value, each member has an incentive to shape it in such a way as to maximize its own value capture—though very few will be in a position to accomplish this. Since a bargaining structure defines a hierarchy of negotiations, I use the term *hierarchy strategy* to denote a firm's approach to optimizing its value capture through the creation of a favorable bargaining structure in its value chain.

Building on the insights from case studies in the home appliance and commercial aircraft industries, I suggest that the two key determinants of bargaining structure are the underlying value chain architecture and the direct action of powerful firms. First, as the value chain architecture circumscribes the division of labor along the value chain it mostly serves as a template for the bargaining structure. Thus, firms can use the value chain architecture and its determinants to create a beneficial bargaining structure. Following Baldwin and Clark (2000), Colfer and Baldwin (2010), and Henderson and Clark (1990), I suggest that firms can leverage the underlying modular product architecture to shape industry architecture, the respective value chain architecture, and, thus, the bargaining structure. Second, firms that are hard to replace have the power to directly influence the bargaining structure without altering the underlying value chain architecture.

The present work contributes to the discussion of the determinants of value capture, in particular, industry architecture. I complement the established bottleneck strategy with the notion of bargaining structure as a lever to enhance value capture. Further, the hierarchical Shapley value complements the existing extensions of the Shapley value in the field of cooperative game theory.

The study is structured as follows: Chapter 2 provides an overview of the relevant literature, both from a business and a game theory perspective; Chapter 3 introduces the

[3] Although an announced royalty rate may differ from the final royalty rate paid, it can be used as an indicator.

notion of bargaining structure and derives the research questions; Chapter 4 analyzes the effect of bargaining structure on value capture using cooperative game theory; Chapter 5 focuses on the determinants of bargaining using case studies in the home appliance and commercial aircraft industry; and Chapter 6 discusses the findings and provides perspectives on managerial implications and limitations.

2 Determinants of value capture

This study focuses on the distribution of value within the value chain, therefore, I follow prior research (Bowman and Ambrosini 2000; Dedrick et al. 2010; Lepak et al. 2007) in defining value—more specifically, "value created"—as the difference between the costs of producing a certain good or providing a certain service and the price that buyers pay for the end product. In this chapter, I review the pertinent literature on value appropriation and bargaining, industry or value chain architecture as a determinant of value capture, and game theory perspectives.

2.1 Profiting from innovation

The literature on profiting from innovation, building on the groundbreaking work of Teece (1986), emphasizes two key factors that determine a firm's value capture: the appropriability regime and the control over complementary assets. The first refers to the ability to protect the innovation from imitation or reproduction through legal mechanisms (e.g., patents, copyrights, trade secrets) and barriers resulting from the nature of the focal technology (e.g., secrecy, tacit knowledge) (Pisano and Teece 2007). The control over complementary assets (e.g., access to input materials, specialized complementary products), on the other hand, refers to assets and capabilities required for a successful commercialization of the innovation.

Naturally, firms aim to leverage these determinants to enhance value capture. Strategies described in the literature are based mostly on the idea of creating a "bottleneck", that is, on becoming the firm most difficult to replace in the value chain[4] (Baldwin 2014; Iansiti and Levien 2004; Jacobides and MacDuffie 2013; Jacobides et al. 2006; Morris and Ferguson 1993; Pisano and Teece 2007). Irreplaceability and inimitability may be due to various isolating mechanisms (Rumelt 1984), in particular causal ambiguity regarding the source of the respective resource and legal property

4 Note that the notion of a bottleneck refers to replaceability relative to the other firms in the value chain, and as a result determines value capture relative to what the value chain as a whole captures. The latter, in contrast, is determined among other things by absolute replaceability by competing, substitutive value chains. That is, even a bottleneck firm might face low value capture in absolute terms if all firms in the value chain, including the bottleneck firm, are easily replaceable.

rights. I refer to the approach to optimizing a firm's value capture by becoming the bottleneck in the value chain as the bottleneck strategy.

A firm can seek to create a bottleneck in different parts of the value chain, either by protecting the core innovation and product, or by having exclusive control of complementary assets. For example, a tight appropriability regime building on strong patent protection, secrecy of core functionalities, or a high level of tacit knowledge, prevents imitation of the core technology and impedes competition. Thus, the firm's contribution to the value creation process becomes valuable, rare, inimitable, and non-substitutable (Barney 1991). In case of weak appropriability regimes innovators can generate returns by leveraging the complementary assets even if the innovation itself does not directly ensure sufficient value capture (Pisano and Teece 2007).

A bottleneck position can significantly enhance bargaining power and value capture (Jacobides et al. 2006). Value is distributed among the firms that contribute to its creation through bargaining (Brandenburger and Stuart 1996); the value share a given firm can appropriate depends on its bargaining power relative to its negotiation partners (Porter 1980). Bargaining power, in turn, is driven by the availability of alternative providers of the same good or substitutes, the replacement costs to be borne by the remaining firms if a firm withdraws from negotiations, the switching costs for the focal firm if it needs to deploy its resources for other purposes, time pressure, and access to relevant information (Buvik and Reve 2002; Dedrick et al. 2010; Porter 1980). That is, bargaining power is driven by the replaceability in the value chain. Hence, a bottleneck position in the value chain (rooted in the focal product or complementary assets) translates into a bottleneck position in negotiations and results in increased value capture.

2.2 Value chain architecture

The literature discusses various approaches to attaining a bottleneck position. Many of these imply changes to industry or value chain architecture, that is, to the nested structure of firms circumscribing the division of labor (Jacobides et al. 2006).

Distinct product solutions designed to satisfy the same customer need might have different value chain architectures. In particular, when a new market emerges, each product design may come with its own organization of the value chain; firms approach market needs and process difficulties differently and there is no common understanding of key performance criteria (Clark 1985). However, when a dominant product design emerges,[5] most firms will adopt the corresponding value chain organization in order to reduce transaction costs. Thus, one or a small number of stable "industry architectures" consisting of several value chains for core and complementing products, emerge in the formative years of an industry, each with its own members (Gawer and Cusumano 2002; Iansiti and Levien 2004).

Industry and value chain architectures can display significant inertia (Pisano and Teece 2007). In particular, when the industry becomes more mature and firms increasingly specialize, switching costs associated with changing the architecture increase. Nevertheless, architectures can change over time, triggered, for example, by significant technological and regulatory changes or demand shifts (Jacobides et al. 2006).

Scholars have studied how firms seek to influence the architecture of their respective value chain and industry for their own benefit with the goal of achieving a bottleneck position (Baldwin and Clark 2000; Chesbrough 2003; Iansiti and Levien 2004; Jacobides et al. 2006; Pisano and Teece 2007). Several studies indicate that innovators, entrepreneurs, and other key firms may be in a position to shape the value chain architecture to achieve a dominant position.

It often requires the collaboration of various firms to bring a product innovation to the market. Having the opportunity to strategically think about and shape the architecture of their value chain, innovators have the ability to decide on the boundaries of their firm, the division of labor along the value chain, and the relationships with suppliers and complementors (Jacobides et al. 2006). These decisions include, among others, whether to make or buy components, how to design interfaces for suppliers and complementors, how to divide roles among potential suppliers, and how to interact with other firms in the value chain. Thus, innovators not only decide on their own role but also have the opportunity to shape their value chain architecture.

Further, Santos and Eisenhardt (2009) show how entrepreneurial firms shape value chain and industry architecture to achieve a dominant position. They observed three mechanisms that entrepreneurs use to set their organization boundaries and demarcate

---

5 According to Abernathy and Utterback (1978), in the beginning of a market product design is in flux as companies vary product characteristics and innovate to best meet the new or emerging needs of customers. Through standardization and focus on efficient production one or a small number of dominant product designs may emerge over time.

nascent markets. First, they aim to claim the market and become the "cognitive referent" through defining and promoting a separate identity for the firm and the market. Second, through the creation of alliances they aim to increase market power and draw a line to nascent markets. Third, over time, entrepreneurs attempt to adapt the boundaries of the firm to the boundaries of the market to reduce the competitive thread.

Last, key individuals can trigger architectural change through the use of their position and assets (e.g., resources, contacts). Ferraro and Gurses (2009) use the example of the U.S. motion picture industry to show how individual firms can leverage exogenous changes—in this case technological change outside the focal industry and governmental legislation—to reshape the value chain and industry architecture. Through linking unconnected domains and expertise, firms can create new opportunities and put themselves in a position to drive architectural change in the industry. Similarly, firms in a keystone position (Iansiti and Levien 2004) have the power to change the value chain architecture. These so-called keystone firms have an important role in the network of firms of an ecosystem[6] and through providing a stable and predictable environment (e.g., a platform) they aim to increase health and value creation throughout the ecosystem. Further, they share a large portion of the value with the rest of the ecosystem to strengthen their position.

Overall, three areas of determinants that can be potentially leveraged for shaping the value chain and industry architecture are discussed in the literature: distribution of capabilities, regulations and norms, and product architecture.

First, as it is the basis for strategic decisions when organizing the value chain, the knowledge and capability endowment of firms has a strong effect on value chain and industry architecture (Ferraro and Gurses 2009; Zirpoli and Camuffo 2009). Technical capabilities determine whether a firm can best produce a particular component in the desired specification. Hence, they influence the division of labor. Firms try to leverage their own capabilities to influence, for example, task partitioning and thus achieve a comfortable position in the value chain and control over suppliers. Technical competences and capabilities can be developed over time, however, this process is slow, uncertain, and costly (Hoetker 2006). Although it is an important strategic activity for

---

6 An ecosystem consists not only of the firms involved in producing a given product but also the firms in the value chains of complementary products.

firms, the development of capabilities is a rather long-term oriented lever to gain an advantage.

Second, the norm-based and legal framework including reputation, regulation, technology, and industry standards are factors that influence value chain architectures (Jacobides and MacDuffie 2013). For example, technical standards are essential for the development and commercialization of some technologies such as mobile communication, as they define interfaces and thus enable compatibility and specialization of firms (Anton and Yao 1995). Defining interface standards implicitly sets the boundaries of modules. Thus, standards foster competition in some parts of the value chain by enabling "plug and play" of modules while they potentially restrict competition in other parts of the technical system (Pisano and Teece 2007). Hence, standards play an important role in the development of the value chain and industry architecture and firms aim to influence them (Jacobides et al. 2006).

Third, product architecture, in particular modular product architecture, affects value chain architecture. Modular product architectures are characterized by a low level of interdependencies among subsystems (Baldwin and Clark 1997; Sanchez and Mahoney 1996; Simon 1962) and therefore enable and shape the division of labor within an industry (Baldwin and Clark 1997; Langlois 2003; Langlois and Robertson 1992; Sturgeon 2002).[7] More precisely, because of the low level of interdependencies, a change in a single subsystem has (almost) no effect on other parts of the system. Coupled with standardized interfaces it allows firms to offer greater product variety with little incremental complexity as modules can easily be exchanged or updated (Sanchez and Mahoney 1996). As modules can be designed and produced independently of the rest of the system, modular product architecture not only shapes and enables the division of labor but also promotes and facilitates the specialization of firms (Colfer and Baldwin 2010; Langlois and Garzarelli 2008). It is important to note that, in this context, the architecture of a newly introduced product is to a good extent under the control of the innovator who may design it purposefully to influence value chain architecture and value capture. In this context, Thomas et al. (2014) highlight the role of platform

---

7 Similarly, focusing on the transactional character of an industry, the coupling between product and supply chain architectures has been noted in the supply chain literature (Lee and Sasser 1995; Simchi-Levi et al. 2008). Further, a source of additional benefits is the concurrent design of product and supply chain architecture, which results in lower costs and greater performance (Gan and Grunow 2013).

architecture and the logic of "architectural leverage." For example, firms can stimulate competition in other segments of the value chain through the design of open interfaces (Eisenmann et al. 2009). At the same time, firms seek to restrict competition in their own fields by strengthening the appropriability regime, for example, through a product design that is modular with regard to intellectual property (Henkel et al. 2013). Hence, firms can leverage product architecture to attain a bottleneck position.

2.3 Game theoretic perspective

Game theory has often been used to shed light on fundamental questions in business strategy: how winners emerge, how to succeed in competition, and how competition affects value capture. The two fields of game theory, cooperative and non-cooperative, approach these questions from different angles. While non-cooperative game theory studies the strategic moves and interactions among a set of players, the cooperative branch focuses on the power of players, possible outcomes and how the payoffs are allocated. Note that the terms "cooperative" and "non-cooperative" can be misleading as cooperative game theory is used to analyze competitive environments as well, and non-cooperative game theory also incorporates cooperative aspects (Brandenburger and Stuart 2007).

Non-cooperative game theory studies the effects of strategies and actions of a player and aims to identify plausible outcomes. However, non-cooperative models require detailed specifications of the process, possible moves and countermoves, and information available to players.[8] The analytical results of a non-cooperative game model heavily depend on the precise specification of the particular setting, the process, and the rules (Aumann and Shapley 1994; Kreps 1990). Therefore, generalization of results is limited to very similar settings (Camerer 1991). Nevertheless, non-cooperative game theory is a powerful tool used to understand the strategic moves of firms.

Cooperative game theory takes a different perspective. It focuses on possible outcomes, studies potential coalitions of players, and how players allocate the value that was generated cooperatively. In particular, cooperative approaches are suitable for situations in which binding contracts among players are made and adhered to (Aumann

---

[8] In the context of Nash equilibrium it is assumed that players are aware of the potential strategies of other players as they observed a similar game beforehand (Gul 1989).

and Shapley 1994). In contrast to non-cooperative game theory, there is no restriction on the process of how players get to the focal setup. It can rather be seen as a free-form interaction between players and hence fits into the realistic business process of value creation and appropriation (Brandenburger and Stuart 1996; Winter 2002).

Both game theories, non-cooperative and cooperative, are relevant for analyzing business settings; however, each takes an individual perspective. Since my research focus is to understand the drivers of value capture without specifying or assuming a particular procedure of how agreements are reached, the use of cooperative game theory is a better fit for this study.

The introduction of cooperative game theory to management literature started with the seminal article by Brandenburger and Stuart (1996), who employed it to develop the added-value concept. Later, MacDonald and Ryall (2004) used a formal cooperative approach to assess how competition and replaceability drive value appropriation and derive strategies for innovators. Furthermore, Brandenburger and Stuart (2007) developed a powerful approach for analyzing business strategies combining non-cooperative and cooperative approaches, so-called biform games. Other contributions are the results of research by Adegbesan (2009), Adner and Zemsky (2006), Bennett (2013), Chatain and Zemsky (2007), Lippman and Rumelt (2003), and Ryall and Sorenson (2007).

The most prominent concepts in cooperative game theory are the Shapley value (Shapley 1953) and the Core (Gillies 1953; Shapley 1952). While the Core theory provides a set of value distributions that no group of players can unilaterally improve upon, the Shapley value provides a single distribution that can be perceived as a "fair" allocation (see Sections 4.1.1 and 4.4 for a detailed discussion of the concepts). The Shapley value is part of the set of acceptable solutions provided by the Core if the game is convex (Shapley 1971), that is, if the participating firms complement each other and create complementarity effects.[9] In the meta-analysis of Michener et al. (1983) covering more than 1,400 observations in six separate studies, the Shapley value consistently

---

[9] That is, the value collectively (created and) captured by the group of firms is larger than the sum of values (created and) captured individually.

showed relatively high predictive accuracy compared to the Core and outperformed all other tested cooperative concepts as well.[10]

Because of its advantageous properties, the Shapley value has been applied in numerous studies. Although it has been extensively used in economics and political sciences, there are, thus far, only a few applications in the field of management studies. Granot and Sošić (2005), among others, use the Shapley value to model the incentive of firms to take part in supply alliances; Layne-Farrar et al. (2007) apply the Shapley value to the pricing of patents in standard setting organizations, suggesting it can be seen as a possible benchmark for fair, reasonable, and non-discriminatory (FRAND) pricing; Hendrikse (2011) uses it to model the distribution of revenues to analyze governance structure changes in the fruit and vegetable business; and, Kattuman et al. (2011) use variance decomposition based on the Shapley value regression to study the influence of corporate groups on affiliate profitability. Further, Cachon and Netessine (2004) and Nagarajan and Sošić (2008) provide an extensive overview of supply chain literature applying the Shapley value.

Further, the Shapley value has a non-cooperative interpretation. Gul (1989) shows that the expected profit from sequential trade, that is, the utility in the equilibrium, is the Shapley value when time intervals between bargaining are arbitrary small. Conversely, a couple of bargaining methods that lead to a value allocation according to the Shapley value have been developed and specified (Inderst and Wey 2001; Pérez-Castrillo and Wettstein 2001).

---

[10] Besides the Shapley value and the Core, Michener et al. (1983) test the Nucleolus, the Disruption Nucleolus, the 2-Center solution, and the Equality solution. In the comparison of different concepts with the Core, the Shapley value is the only concept that in all tests shows a significant higher predictive accuracy. Predictive accuracy is indicated by the mean goodness-of-fit score. For imputation theories, that is, theories that suggest a point solution, goodness-of-fit scores measure the Euclidian distance between the observed and predicted results. In addition, the goodness-of-fit score used for the Core takes the size of the predicted solution space into account.

3 Bargaining structure

I begin this chapter with an introduction of the notion of bargaining structure, which leads to the derivation of the research questions that aim to understand its determinants and effects.

3.1 Hierarchy in negotiations: Bargaining structure

When several parties have to split a given value, one or more individual negotiations may take place. For example, the parties may be divided into two groups, and the distribution of value between them is negotiated by representatives from each group. The value obtained by each group is split in further negotiations between the members of the respective group. In the present context, I define the *bargaining structure* of the overall value distribution process as a division of the set of players into disjoint subsets, each of which may, in turn, be divided into disjoint subsets, and so on until all lowest-level subsets contain only one party.[11] This definition is in line with the notion of bargaining structure used in the literature on interpersonal bargaining ranging back to Krauss (1966). It was mostly examined in the context of union and wage bargaining, for example, in Calmfors et al. (1988) and Moene et al. (1993).

Such hierarchical negotiations will be present in most real-life value chains, with the exception of very simple cases and vertically integrated value chains. With large numbers of participating firms, in particular, bargaining will generally be a hierarchical, multi-stage process, to reduce transaction cost (Williamson 1985; Williamson 1991). The manufacturer of the final good will negotiate with its tier-one suppliers; these firms, in turn, will negotiate with their own suppliers. For complex products, this chain of negotiations may continue for several more stages. It will, in general, have no clearly defined end point, since even suppliers of raw materials have their own suppliers of machinery. For the purpose of my analysis, I define the value chain as those firms that provide inputs to production steps that are either close to the final product or specific to

[11] Implicit in this definition is the assumption that each party participates at only one point in the bargaining structure. If a firm participates in several stages of the value chain, and thus in multiple negotiations, the focal firm can be considered a set of different, though linked, positions in the bargaining structure.

it. Since adding an additional tier does not affect the distribution of value in the tiers above, the choice of which tiers to include is not critical to the analysis.

Importantly in this context, a given set of parties may conduct negotiations under different bargaining structures. For example, a final goods manufacturer may buy its inputs directly from a large number of suppliers, or may alternatively choose some of them as tier-one suppliers that provide entire integrated subsystems and that are, in turn, each supplied by a subset of the other suppliers. Also, an individual firm may be positioned in the top tier, supplying directly to the manufacturer, or may deliver its goods to some intermediate integrator.

3.2 Drivers and effects of bargaining structure

To my knowledge, while scholars have focused on how firms can influence their own and others' replaceability in a given bargaining structure to create a bottleneck, the bargaining structure itself has not received any attention as a potential lever for enhancing value capture. As bargaining structure determines the participants of each negotiation, and as value capture in a specific negotiation depends on each party's bargaining power relative to that of thc others, I suggest that the value distribution that eventually results depends on the bargaining structure.

Anticipating this fact, each firm has an incentive to shape the bargaining structure in such a way as to maximize its own value capture. Since a bargaining structure defines a hierarchy of negotiations, the hierarchy strategy denotes a firm's approach to optimizing its value capture through creating a favorable bargaining structure in its value chain.

If bargaining structure matters for value capture, one needs to ask what, in turn, determines bargaining structure. I argue that value chain architecture and individual participants' power are the key determinants, and address them in turn.

As the architecture of a value chain or industry circumscribes the division of labor and roles of firms that participate in producing the product (Jacobides et al. 2006), it outlines as well the transactions of goods and provision of services from upstream to downstream firms. Transactions, in turn, are governed by contracts. The term "contract" is not necessarily to be understood in a legal sense but more generally as explicit or implicit agreements and understandings between firms.[12] Hence, the value chain architecture gives rise to a transaction related contract structure, that is, the network of contracts between firms governing the exchange of goods and provision of services.[13]

The terms of transaction related contracts include the price, thus directly determining the distribution of value. As they are commonly subject to negotiations (Nagarajan and Sošić 2008), the transaction related contract structure entails the bargaining structure making the value chain architecture one of its key determinants. Consequently, firms in a position to control value chain architecture—for example, using product architecture to shape value chain architecture—can use this power to change the bargaining structure to their advantage and implement a hierarchy strategy to enhance value capture.

In addition, some firms might have the power, based on their assets (e.g., resources, contacts) or position in the industry, to shape the bargaining structure directly. For example, automotive OEMs in some cases use their power and negotiate directly with a tier-2 supplier while leaving aside the respective tier-1 supplier, despite its place in the value chain architecture (MacDuffie and Helper 2007). In such a case, the OEM does not change the role of the tier-1 supplier in the value chain architecture—the tier-1 supplier remains responsible for the subsystem and its integration –, but it does modify the bargaining structure. Further, in the beginning of an industry, innovators have the freedom to decide on the relationships with suppliers and downstream firms and thus can directly shape bargaining structure.

All in all, these questions are the core of my research and are the focus of this dissertation. In short, the research questions are:

- Does bargaining structure affect value capture?
- What are the key drivers of bargaining structure?
- To what extent does bargaining structure mirror value chain architecture?
- Do firms actively manage the bargaining structure? What levers do they apply?

---

12 The net of transaction related contracts is part of what Alchian and Demsetz (1972) and Baldwin and Clark (2000) call contract structure.

13 Note that a contract can cover more than one transaction and, in rare cases, involves more than two parties. Thus, there might not be a one-to-one mapping between transaction and transaction related contract structure. Alchian and Demsetz (1972) point out that for team development and production, the creation of a central common party, a firm, in combination with bilateral contracts between the central party and the individual input owners is more efficient than a multilateral contract.

- If firms actively manage the bargaining structure, is their actions are in line with the hierarchy strategy?

In the following chapters, I apply two different methods to examine the research questions. In Chapter 4, I use cooperative game theory to understand the effect of bargaining structure on value capture and derive rules that help determine which bargaining structure is the most beneficial for a given firm. In Chapter 5, I evaluate case studies to shed light on the questions of whether and how firms influence bargaining structures.

4 Modeling the effect of bargaining structure on value capture

In order to understand value appropriation in a value chain, I model the bargaining over value as a cooperative game among the participating firms. As indicated in Section 2.3, a cooperative model is the best game theoretic approach for this research as it does not restrict the analysis to a mode of interaction among firms and a particular procedure of bargaining but assumes binding contracts. The following analysis is limited to value distribution under a given bargaining structure. The selection of firms that contribute to value creation, the cost of production, and the value that the value chain as a whole captures on the market are taken as given. The goal of this approach is to understand to what extent bargaining structure drives value capture and to derive strategies to enhance it.

In the first part of the chapter, I introduce the cooperative model that is used in the latter sections to evaluate and compare bargaining structures. While Section 4.2 derives insights from basic bargaining structures, Section 4.3 extents the model to incorporate system integrators and inputs provided under perfect competition or an open source license. At the end of the chapter, I open up the discussion to other cooperative solution concepts and examine to what extent they support the results. A glossary of terms for this section can be found in Appendix A.

4.1 The basic model

In this section, the game theoretic model is introduced. Starting with the Shapley value for non-hierarchical bargaining structures, I will derive a new solution concept that is appropriate to reflect hierarchy in bargaining structures.

4.1.1 Non-hierarchical value distribution

Since the theory of cooperative games is well covered in literature I will build in the following on an existing concept, namely the Shapley value (Shapley 1953). The Shapley value (SV) provides a prediction of a player's value capture in a situation of bargaining over the distribution of a fixed value. It is based on the player's average marginal contribution to all possible subsets (or coalitions) of players, in all possible orderings. In contrast to other solution concepts such as the Core,[14] the SV provides point estimates for the distribution, has a relatively high predictive accuracy (Michener et al. 1983; Michener et al. 1987), and is the only solution concept for cooperative games that has a number of desirable and plausible properties, which will be discussed later.

Formally, a value chain with the set $M = \{m_j\}_{j=1,\dots,n}, n \in \mathbb{N}$ of bargaining firms is considered. For the time being, I introduce the simplifying assumption that every firm participates only once in the bargaining structure.

The characteristic function $v: 2^M \to \mathbb{R}$ with $v(\emptyset) = 0$ assigns to every subset of firms $J \subseteq M$ a value $v(J)$. For the focal model, let $v(J)$ be the stand-alone value of the group of firms J, that is, the value that the focal group could capture (more precisely, generate and capture) jointly without any other firm participating in the value chain (e.g., through selling an intermediate product to other firms or customers). Thus, v not only takes the value add of a firm from a product/ consumer perspective into account, but also its replaceability in the value chain.

Further, a group of firms (or even a full value chain or bargaining structure) is called complementary if for any subgroup of firms the value created (and captured) collectively is larger than (or equal to) the sum of values of any partition. That is, $v(J \cup K) \geq v(J) + v(K)$ for all $J, K \subseteq M$ with $J \cap K = \emptyset$. The difference between the value created collectively and the sum of the individually created values is denoted as the complementarity effect.

An extreme case of complementarity is essentiality. A firm is called essential if it is indispensable in the bargaining structure in the sense that the other firms in the value chain would not obtain any value without it. Essentiality in the context of the focal model corresponds to a bottleneck position in the value chain. As discussed in Section 2.2, it is rooted in the endowment with assets and capabilities that are critical for value creation and capture, such as the exclusive access to customers or unique knowledge for producing a critical component. In reality, firms are often rather nearly than fully essential as some kind of workaround (more or less costly) is available in most cases. However, to carve out the effect of bargaining structures, full essentiality, which is the

[14] Other solution concepts including their differences to the Shapley value will be discussed in Section 4.4.

continuous extension of "difficult to replace", will be considered. Formally, the essential firms in the value chain constitute a set C_e such that $v(J) = 0$ if $C_e \nsubseteq J$.

In contrast, a firm in perfect competition does not capture any value as it is easily replaceable. Nevertheless, such a firm, supplying, for example, a commodity good, has a relevant position in the value chain as it increases the value of the overall product. For the moment, I assume that none of the firms participating in the value chain and bargaining structure is in perfect competition. In Section 4.3.2, the notion of non-value-appropriating firms is introduced to include perfect (or strong) competition and inputs under open source licenses.

If all firms are on the same hierarchical level in the bargaining structure, that is, they bargain jointly (or in bilateral negotiations, for example, the final product manufacturer with tier-1 suppliers),[15] the standard SV can be used to predict the value distribution. The estimated value appropriation of a player $m_j \in M$ is given by

$$\phi_{m_j}(v) := \sum_{S \subseteq M \setminus \{m_j\}} \frac{|S|!\,(n - |S| - 1)!}{n!} \Big(v\big(S \cup \{m_j\}\big) - v(S)\Big). \tag{1}$$

That is, the value capture $\phi_{m_j}(v)$ of a firm $m_j \in M$ is determined by the value add of m_j to every possible subset $S \subseteq M \setminus \{m_j\}$, weighted by a factor that takes the permutation of firms in S into account.

As indicated, the Shapley value satisfies some desirable properties (Shapley 1953), namely:

- Efficiency: $\sum_{m_j \in M} \phi_{m_j}(v) = v(M)$, that is, the sum of the value capture of all firms equals the value capture of the overall value chain.

---

15 Under the assumption that every firm has transparency on the other firms, it is plausible that bilateral negotiations result in a similar value split. In reality, not only the central firm in bilateral negotiations, which makes bilateral agreements with each of the other firms, knows about the value-add of others, but mostly every firm has a (more or less precise) estimate. Non-central firms may even communicate among each other. As, all firms can assess their value-add to any subgroup, the central firm is not necessarily the firm enabling (or restricting) joint value creation (such as a system integrator as discussed in Section 4.3.1). Thus, the value distribution is most likely the same as in joint negotiations.

- Symmetry: symmetric firms in terms of value add receive the same share of value of the total value chain, that is, if $v(m_j \cup J) = v(m_k \cup J)$ for all $J \subseteq M \backslash \{m_j, m_k\}$, then $\phi_{m_j}(v) = \phi_k(v)$ holds.
- Additivity: combining two cooperative games yields a new game described by the sum of the two original characteristic functions, that is, for two characteristic functions $v, w: 2^M \to \mathbb{R}$ with $(v+w)(J) = v(J) + w(J)$ for all $J \subseteq M$, the Shapley value is as well additive, that is, $\phi_{m_j}(v+w) = \phi_{m_j}(v) + \phi_{m_j}(w) \; \forall m_j \in M$.
- Invariance under dummy players: firms with no value add do not capture any value, that is, for a dummy firm $m_j \in M$ with $v(J \cup m_j) - v(J) = 0 \; \forall J \subset M$, it holds that $\phi_{m_j}(v) = 0$.

4.1.2 The hierarchical Shapley value

In the following, I consider a hierarchical bargaining structure, which, for simplicity, is restricted to two levels. The set of participating firms is divided into $k \in \mathbb{N}$ subsets, the representatives of which bargain in a top-level (L1) negotiation. These subsets are referred to as clusters. Subsequently, the members of each cluster bargain among each other in level two (L2) negotiations to split their respective group's bounty.

The representative of a cluster in top-level negotiations may be an independent neutral firm or one of the firms that are part of the cluster. As both are incentivized to maximize value capture in top-level negotiations, the question who represents the cluster does not affect value distribution. Further, the additional knowledge of the representative on top-level negotiations does not provide an advantage for value distribution within the cluster. First, I assume that firms in a given cluster can verify the value capture of their cluster in top-level negotiations and the representative would be easily replaceable.[16] Second, all firms in a cluster assume the rest of the value chain being in place. This point will be detailed in the next paragraph.

I propose a generalization of the SV to predict value distribution in such two-level bargaining structures. The *Hierarchical Shapley value* (HSV) describes a step-wise

---

16 Thus, the negotiator will not capture any (additional) value – as will be discuss in Section 4.3.2.

value distribution that, in both steps, follows the classical SV. For firms in a given L2 negotiation, it assumes limited transparency insofar as they only know each other's value add and bargaining power, but not that of firms in other clusters. In an L2 negotiation, participants assume that all other clusters are complete and in place.[17] In this respect, the HSV differs from the otherwise similar solution concept to hierarchical negotiations introduced by Owen (1977).

Formally, the definition of coalition structures by Aumann and Drèze (1974) serves as a basis to model hierarchical bargaining structures. A hierarchical bargaining structure is a partition $\mathfrak{B} = \{M_i\}_{i\in\{1,\dots,k\}}$ of the set M of firms into k clusters M_i such that $M = \bigcup_{i=1}^{k} M_i$ (the elements of $\mathfrak{B}$ cover M), and $M_i \cap M_j = \emptyset \ \forall M_i, M_j \in \mathfrak{B}: i \neq j$ (the elements of $\mathfrak{B}$ are pairwise disjoint).

To apply a SV distribution for L1 bargaining, the induced characteristic function $\hat{v}$ is defined for a set of clusters $J \subseteq \mathfrak{B}$ as

$$\hat{v}: 2^{\mathfrak{B}} \to \mathbb{R}, \qquad \hat{v}(J) := v\left(\bigcup_{M_i \in J} M_i\right). \tag{2}$$

Consequently, the L1-HSV of a cluster $M_i \in \mathfrak{B}$ is given by

$$\phi_{M_i}(\hat{v}, \mathfrak{B}) := \sum_{S \subseteq \mathfrak{B}\setminus\{M_i\}} \frac{|S|!\,(k - |S| - 1)!}{k!} \big(\hat{v}(S \cup M_i) - \hat{v}(S)\big). \tag{3}$$

For value distribution on L2, that is, within a cluster M_i, I define for each $M_i \in \mathfrak{B}$ the induced characteristic function $\check{v}_{M_i}: 2^{M_i} \to \mathbb{R}$. For $J \subseteq M_i$, let

$$\check{v}_{M_i}(J) := \frac{\big(v(J \cup (M\setminus M_i)) - v(M\setminus M_i)\big)}{v(M) - v(M\setminus M_i)} \phi_{M_i}(\hat{v}, \mathfrak{B}). \tag{4}$$

---

17 This assumption is sensible and even required, if the firms' contributions are characterized by complementarities. For example, the value of a laptop screen as a stand-alone product would be zero due to strong complementarities with the other parts of the computer. Thus, the firms that contribute to production of the screen (which form a cluster) would negotiate their value distribution assuming the rest of the computer to be complete. Further, this idea is in line with the information hiding principle of modular product architectures (Baldwin and Clark 2000), which is a driver of value chain architecture and bargaining structure.

The L2-HSV for a firm $m_j \in M_i$ is then given by

$$\phi_{m_j}^{HSV}(\check{v}_{M_i}, \mathfrak{B}) := \sum_{S \subseteq M_i \setminus \{m_j\}} \frac{|S|!\,(|M_i| - |S| - 1)!}{|M_i|!} (\check{v}_{M_i}(S \cup \{m_j\}) - \check{v}_{M_i}(S)). \quad (5)$$

For simplicity, I use $\phi_{m_j}^{HSV}(v)$ to refer to the value capture $\phi_{m_j}^{HSV}(\check{v}_{M_i}, \mathfrak{B})$ of a firm m_j in a hierarchical bargaining structure $\mathfrak{B}$, that is, $\phi_{m_j}^{HSV}(v) := \phi_{m_j}^{HSV}(\check{v}_{M_i}, \mathfrak{B})$. As $\check{v}_{M_i}$ is based on the characteristic function v, the value capture $\phi_{m_j}^{HSV}(\check{v}_{M_i}, \mathfrak{B})$ is also a function of v.

The HSV satisfies some favorable properties, as the following proposition shows:

PROPOSITION 1: *The HSV, defined according Equation (5), satisfies the following properties: efficiency, invariance under dummy players, symmetry across coalitions and symmetry within coalitions. However, as the HSV is defined as a quotient, it inhibits additivity of the operator.*

See Appendix B for details and the proof of the properties.

Thus, the following holds true: the value capture of a cluster M_i equals the sum of the value capture of all firms that are part of M_i.

$$\sum_{m_j \in M_i} \phi_{m_j}^{HSV}(\check{v}_{M_i}, \mathfrak{B}) = \check{v}_{M_i}(M_i) = \phi_{M_i}(\hat{v}, \mathfrak{B})$$

Although the HSV could be generalized to multi-level bargaining structures, I constrain the analysis to bi-level structures.

4.2 Results

In the following, I will analyze the effect of hierarchical and non-hierarchical bargaining structures on value capture and derive recommendations how the hierarchy strategy can help firms to enhance value appropriation. Applying the model introduced in the preceding section, I start with a basic three-firm model that will be extended in terms of number of firms involved.

Note that integration of inputs from different firms is not explicitly considered. Integration enables complementarity, that is, without integration the value of a group of inputs equals the sum of the values. For the moment, I assume that every firm can perform the integration or the integration service is in competitive supply. Further, it is assumed that none of the firms is in perfect competition, that is, there are no easily available substitutes. In Section 4.3 these assumptions will be relaxed.

4.2.1 Three-firm bargaining structures

First, I analyze the general three-firm case with $M = \{m_1, m_2, m_3\}$. The hierarchical bargaining structure is given by $\mathfrak{B} = \{\{m_1, m_2\}, \{m_3\}\}$, that is, m_1 and m_2 form a cluster. For simplicity, I use the notation m_j, $m_j m_k$, and $m_j m_k m_l$ instead of $\{m_j\}$, $\{m_j, m_k\}$, $\{m_j, m_k, m_l\}$ for $m_j, m_k, m_l \in M$. Figure 1 illustrates the non-hierarchical and hierarchical bargaining structures. Firms or clusters of firms that participate in the same negotiation are marked through a dashed box. A vertical line connecting a negotiation of firms on the lower level with a box on the top-level indicates that the focal firms are part of a cluster that is represented in top-level negotiations.

Using the definitions of the SV and the HSV introduced earlier, it is straightforward to calculate, for the single L1 firm (m_3), the difference between both as

$$\phi_{m_3}^{HSV}(v) - \phi_{m_3}(v)$$
$$= \frac{1}{6}\big(v(m_1 m_2 m_3) - v(m_1 m_2) - v(m_1 m_3) - v(m_2 m_3) + v(m_1) \qquad (6)$$
$$+ v(m_2) + v(m_3)\big)$$

Introducing the *complementarity gains* $\Delta_{J,K} := v(J \cup K) - v(J) - v(K)$ with $J, K \subseteq M$ and $J \cap K = \emptyset$, and $\Delta_{J,K,L} := v(J \cup K \cup L) - v(J) - v(K) - v(L)$ with $J, K, L \subseteq M$ and being pairwise disjoint, the results above can be rephrased as follows:

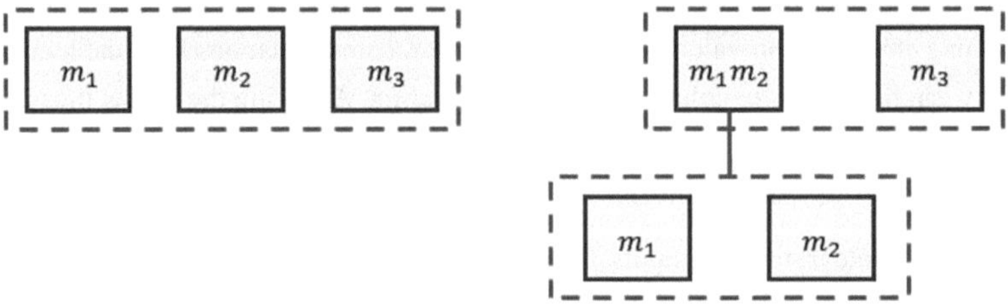

Figure 1: Illustration of non-hierarchical and hierarchical three-firm bargaining structure

$$\phi_{m_3}^{HSV}(v) - \phi_{m_3}(v) = \frac{1}{6}\left(\Delta_{(m_1 \cup m_2),m_3} - \Delta_{m_1,m_3} - \Delta_{m_2 m_3}\right), \tag{7}$$

$$\phi_{m_3}^{HSV}(v) - \phi_{m_3}(v) = \frac{1}{6}\left(\Delta_{m_1,m_2,m_3} - \Delta_{m_1,m_2} - \Delta_{m_1,m_3} - \Delta_{m_2 m_3}\right). \tag{8}$$

Thus, the following proposition is obtained:

PROPOSITION 2: *Being the single L1 firm in a hierarchical three-firm bargaining structure is superior to being in a non-hierarchical bargaining structure if and only if the focal firm's top-level complementarity gains* $\boldsymbol{\Delta_{(m_1 \cup m_2),m_3}}$ *exceed the sum of possible cluster complementarity gains between the focal firm and each of the other firms. An equivalent condition is that the system-level complementarity gains* Δ_{m_1,m_2,m_3} *exceed the sum of the three subsystem complementarity gains.*

Hence, a firm tends to benefit from a single position in top-level negotiations if top-level complementarity is high. In return, if most complementarity is realized within a cluster, that is, in the combination of any two firms, having a direct position in top-level negotiations hurts value capture.

The condition for m_1 (and similarly for m_2) to benefit from a hierarchical bargaining structure is more complicated and not particularly insightful. Firm m_1 benefits from hierarchy if $\left(v(M) + v(m_1 m_2) - v(m_3)/2\left(v(M) - v(m_3)\right)\right)\left(v(M) + v(m_1 m_3) - v(m_2 m_3) - v(m_3)\right) > \frac{1}{3}(2v(M) + v(m_1 m_2) + v(m_1 m_3) - 2v(m_2 m_3) + 2v(m_1) - v(m_2) - v(m_3))$.

To flesh out this result, a specific three-firm bargaining situation characterized by symmetry among non-essential firms is analyzed in the following. That is, the characteristic function depends only on the number of non-essential firms in its argument: $|J| = |J'| \Rightarrow v(C_e \cup J) = v(C_e \cup J')$ for $J, J' \subseteq M \backslash C_e$ with C_e being the set of essential firms. Let E denote an essential and N a non-essential firm. For abbreviation, $\{E, N, N\}$ will be denoted by ENN. Further, let $0 < \alpha \leq \beta \leq 1$ and the characteristic function v be defined according to Table 1. By analyzing the hierarchical and non-hierarchical bargaining structures with different numbers of essential firms, using SV (Table 2) and HSV (Table 3) respectively one can derive the following results (based on the constraints developed in Table 4).

# of essential firms in *M*	Characteristic function $v(J)$ for $J \subseteq M$		
0	$v(N) = \alpha$	$v(NN) = \beta$	$v(NNN) = 1$
1	$v(E) = \alpha$	$v(EN) = \beta$	$v(ENN) = 1$
2	$v(E) = 0$	$v(EE) = \beta$	$v(EEN) = 1$
3	$v(E) = 0$	$v(EE) = 0$	$v(EEE) = 1$

Table 1: Characteristic function for three-firm bargaining structure with varying number of essential and non-essential symmetric firms

# of essential firms in *M*	$\phi_E(v)$	$\phi_N(v)$
0	-	$1/3$
1	$(1 + \alpha + \beta)/3$	$(2 - \alpha - \beta)/6$
2	$(2 + \beta)/6$	$(1 - \beta)/3$
3	$1/3$	-

Table 2: Value capture of essential and non-essential symmetric firms in a non-hierarchical three-firm bargaining structure

# ess. firms in		L1-HSV of...		L2-HSV of firms in m_1m_2	
m_1m_2	m_3	m_1m_2	m_3	Essential	Non-essential
0	0	$\frac{1}{2}(1-\alpha+\beta)$	$\frac{1}{2}(1+\alpha-\beta)$	-	$\frac{1}{4}(1-\alpha+\beta)$
1	0	$\frac{1}{2}(1+\beta)$	$\frac{1}{2}(1-\beta)$	$\frac{1}{4}(1+\beta)^2$	$\frac{1}{4}(1-\beta^2)$
0	1	$\frac{1}{2}(1-\alpha)$	$\frac{1}{2}(1+\alpha)$	-	$\frac{1}{4}(1-\alpha)$
2	0	$\frac{1}{2}(1+\beta)$	$\frac{1}{2}(1-\beta)$	$\frac{1}{4}(1+\beta)$	-
1	1	$\frac{1}{2}$	$\frac{1}{2}$	$\frac{1}{4}(1+\beta)$	$\frac{1}{4}(1-\beta)$
2	1	$\frac{1}{2}$	$\frac{1}{2}$	$\frac{1}{4}$	-

Table 3: Value capture of clusters, essential, and non-essential symmetric firms in the three-firm hierarchical bargaining structure

# of essential firms in		Who gains and who loses through a hierarchical bargaining structure
m_1m_2	m_3	
0	0	Firms $\boldsymbol{m_1}$ and $\boldsymbol{m_2}$ gain if and only if $\frac{1}{4}(1-\alpha+\beta)>\frac{1}{3} \Leftrightarrow \beta-\alpha>\frac{1}{3}$, this is if and only if the value add of the second firm is larger than $\frac{1}{3}$.
1	0	The **essential firm in $\boldsymbol{m_1m_2}$** gains if and only if $\frac{1}{4}(1+\beta)^2>\frac{1}{3}(1+\alpha+\beta) \Leftrightarrow \alpha<\frac{1}{4}(\beta+1)(3\beta-1)$. This is only possible if $\beta>\frac{1}{3}$ and $\beta-\alpha>\frac{1}{4}(1-\beta)$ (necessary constraints).

		The **non-essential firm in $\boldsymbol{m_1 m_2}$** gains if and only if $\frac{1}{4}(1-\beta^2) > \frac{1}{6}(2-\alpha-\beta) \Leftrightarrow \alpha > \frac{3}{2}\beta^2 - \beta + \frac{1}{2}$. This is only possible if $0 > (6\beta-2)(\beta-1)$ (as $\alpha \leq \beta$), so if $\beta > \frac{1}{3}$ (necessary constraint). The **non-essential firm $\boldsymbol{m_3}$** gains if and only if $\frac{1}{2}(1-\beta) > \frac{1}{6}(2-\alpha-\beta) \Leftrightarrow 1-\beta > \beta-\alpha$, this is if and only if the value add is larger in the second step (from two to three firms) than in the first step (for every two firms).
0	1	Firms in $\boldsymbol{m_1 m_2}$ gain if and only if $\frac{1}{4}(1-\alpha) > \frac{1}{6}(2-\alpha-\beta) \Leftrightarrow \beta-\alpha > 1-\beta$, this is if and only if the value add is larger in the first step (for every two firms) than in the second step (from two to three firms).
2	0	$\boldsymbol{m_1}$ and $\boldsymbol{m_2}$ gain if and only if $\frac{1}{4}(1+\beta) > \frac{1}{6}(2+\beta) \Leftrightarrow \beta > 1$. Hence, they can never gain through hierarchy.
1	1	The **essential firm in $\boldsymbol{m_1 m_2}$** gains if and only if $\frac{1}{4}(1+\beta) > \frac{1}{6}(2+\beta) \Leftrightarrow \beta > 1$. Hence, the essential firm in $m_1 m_2$ can never gain through hierarchy. The **non-essential firm in $\boldsymbol{m_1 m_2}$** gains if and only if $\frac{1}{4}(1-\beta) > \frac{1}{3}(1-\beta) \Leftrightarrow \beta > 1$. Hence, the non-essential firm in $m_1 m_2$ can never gain through hierarchy.
2	1	Firms $\boldsymbol{m_1}$ and $\boldsymbol{m_2}$ gain if and only if $\frac{1}{4} > \frac{1}{3}$. Hence, m_1 and m_2 can never gain through hierarchy.

Table 4: Analysis of a three-firm bargaining structures: Which firms benefit from a hierarchical bargaining structure (compared to a non-hierarchical one)?

First, if there are no essential firms in the bargaining structure, then the single L1 firm (m_3) benefits from a hierarchical bargaining structure (compared to a non-hierarchical bargaining structure) if the value add of any second firm, for example, the value add of m_3 to m_1 (and vice versa because of symmetry), is less than 1/3 of the overall value to be distributed.[18] Conversely, if there is sufficiently large complementarity between any two firms, they can increase value capture by joining forces in L1 negotiations and creating a joint cluster.

Second, if m_3 is the only essential firm, it benefits from hierarchy if the value add of a second firm joining m_3 in the value chain is smaller than the value add of a third firm joining m_3 and a non-essential firm—in other words, if the top-level complementarity gains exceed those on the cluster level, or $1 - \beta > \beta - \alpha$.

Third, if m_1 is the only essential firm then a) m_1 gains through hierarchy if $\alpha < \frac{1}{4}(\beta + 1)(3\beta - 1)$, b) m_2 gains if $\alpha > \frac{3}{2}\beta^2 - \beta + \frac{1}{2}$, c) m_3 gains if $\alpha > 2\beta - 1$ (Figure 2). Hence, although m_1 and m_2 form a joint cluster, they cannot both benefit from a hierarchical bargaining structure. If m_1 gains, m_2 loses through hierarchy and vice versa. Further, if the essential firm m_1 has a high stand-alone value (α large), it benefits from hierarchy if the value add of a second firm ($\beta - \alpha$) is larger than half of the residual value to be distributed, that is if complementarity decreases. Otherwise both non-essential firms benefit from hierarchy.

Finally, if there are two or more essential firms, an essential firm loses from hierarchy if it is clustered with another firm on L1. Obviously, additional firms in a cluster with one essential firm do not improve the cluster's position in L1 negotiations if other essential firms are involved in top-level negotiations.

When relaxing the assumption of symmetry among non-essential firms, the statements remain valid (see Appendix D).

---

[18] This proposition can be generalized for the n-firm system: In a bargaining structure with only non-essential firms it is beneficial to be in a two-firm cluster if and only if $\alpha_{n-1} - \alpha_1 > \frac{n-2}{n}$ with $\alpha_j :=$ $v(J)$ for $|J| = j$ given all other firms are not clustered. See Appendix C for the proof.

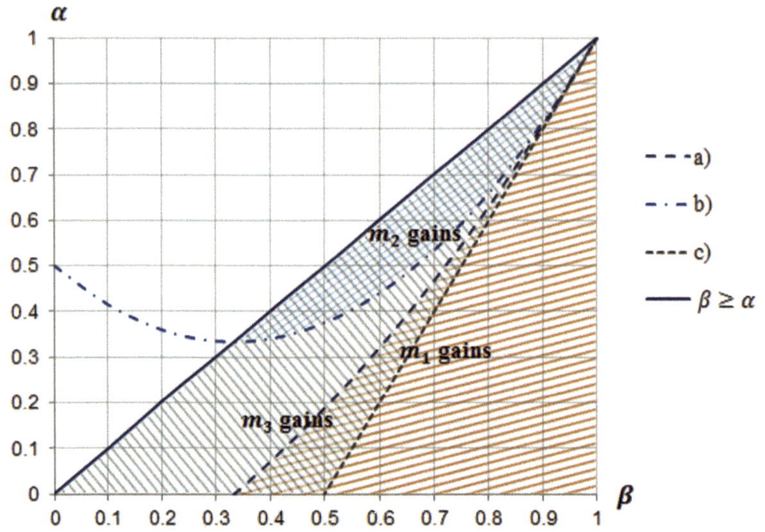

Figure 2: Analysis of three-firm bargaining structures with one essential firm: Which firms benefit from hierarchy?

Overall, the results suggest the following proposition:

PROPOSITION 3: *In the case of three firms, a hierarchical bargaining structure benefits participants in those negotiations in which the highest complementary effects are realized. Consequently, in value chains consisting of several firms being essential for value creation (and capture) the preferred strategy for any firm is to have a single position in top-level negotiations.*

4.2.2 N-firm bargaining structures

The basic three-firm bargaining structure is now extended to $n \in \mathbb{N}$ firms. First, I focus on a numerical analysis of bargaining structures with a single essential firm and strict increasing complementarity. In the latter part of this section, the findings from the numerical analysis are analytically proofed and generalized to arbitrary characteristic functions.

Let again the essential firm be denoted by E and the non-essential firms by $N_1, \dots, N_{n-1}$. In addition, let $\mathfrak{B} = \{M_i\}_{i=1,\dots,k}$ be the clusters of firms. I model complementarity among firms in the value chain through the characteristic function $v(J) = |J|^x$ for $J \subseteq M$ with $E \in J$ and $x > 1$, and $v(J) = 0$ for $J \subseteq M$ with $E \notin J$.

In addition to a non-hierarchical structure a multitude of alternative two-level bargaining structures can be generated through varying the number of clusters as well as the number of firms within each cluster. In order to get a basic understanding I will focus on the extreme cases illustrated in Figure 3.

In the basic non-hierarchical case, the essential firm E captures $\phi_E(v) = \frac{1}{n}\sum_{j=1}^{n} j^x$ according to the SV, while every non-essential firm captures $\phi_{N_1/\ldots/N_{n-1}}(v) = \frac{n^x - \frac{1}{n}\sum_{j=1}^{n} j^x}{n-1}$. Table 5 provides the value distributions for the five focal hierarchical bargaining structures according to the HSV.

As the overall value generated increases with the number of firms in the value chain, the difference between a firm's value appropriation in a given hierarchical and the non-hierarchical bargaining structure relative to the overall value $v(M)$ is the relevant measure. Therefore, let Δ_m^{HSV} be defined as $\Delta_m^{HSV} := \frac{(\phi_m^{HSV}(v) - \phi_m(v))}{v(M)}$ for a firm $m \in M$. A positive value of Δ_m^{HSV} indicates that the focal firm can capture a larger share of the overall value in the hierarchical than in the non-hierarchical bargaining structure. In the following, in the numerical analysis conducted with MATLAB, small to large bargaining structures ranging from three to one million firms are considered. In addition,

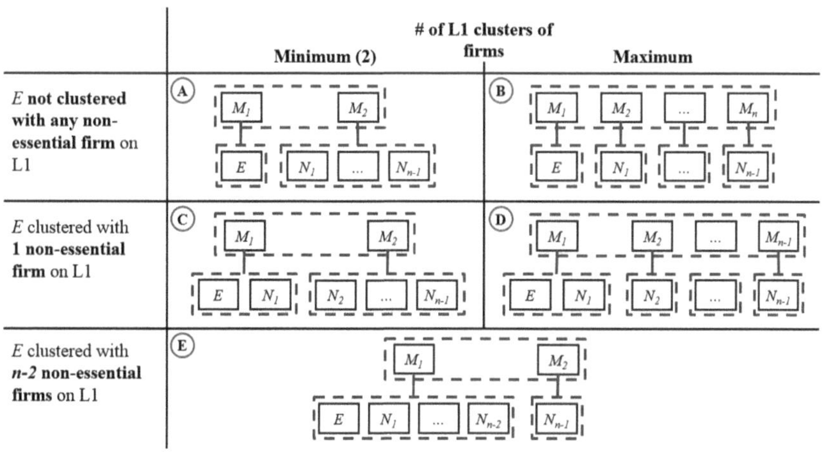

Figure 3: Illustration of two-level hierarchical bargaining structures with one essential and n-1 non-essential firms

Hierarchical bargaining structure	HSV
A	$\phi_E^{HSV}(v) = (n^x + 1)/2$ $\phi_{N_1/\ldots/N_{n-1}}^{HSV}(v) = (n^x - 1)/\,(2(n-1))$
B	Analog to SSV
C	$\phi_E^{HSV}(v) = \frac{(n-1)^x + n^x}{2n^x} \frac{2^x + n^x}{2}$ $\phi_{N_1}^{HSV}(v) = \frac{n^x - (n-1)^x}{2n^x} \frac{2^x + n^x}{2}$ $\phi_{N_2/\ldots/N_{n-1}}^{HSV}(v) = \frac{n^x - 2^x}{2(n-2)}$
D	$\phi_E^{HSV}(v) = \frac{(n-1)^x + n^x}{2n^x(n-1)} \sum_{j=0}^{n-2}(j+2)^x$ $\phi_{N_1}^{HSV}(v) = \left(1 - \frac{(n-1)^x + n^x}{2n^x}\right) \frac{1}{n-1} \sum_{j=0}^{n-2}(j+2)^x$ $\phi_{N_2/\ldots/N_{n-1}}^{HSV}(v) = \frac{1}{n-2}\left(n^x - \frac{1}{n-1}\sum_{j=0}^{n-2}(j+2)^x\right)$
E	$\phi_E^{HSV}(v) = \frac{(n-1)^x + n^x}{2n^x(n-1)} \sum_{j=0}^{n-2}(j+2)^x$ $\phi_{N_1/\ldots/N_{n-2}}^{HSV}(v) = \frac{(n-1)^x + n^x}{2(n-2)}\ (1 - \frac{1}{(n-1)n^x} \sum_{j=0}^{n-2}(j+2)^x)$ $\phi_{N_{n-1}}^{HSV}(v) = (n^x - (n-1)^x)/2$

Table 5: HSV for hierarchical bargaining structures with one essential and n-1 non-essential firms

the level of complementarity varies on a realistic level ($1 < x \leq 3$) but as well differences for value chains with very high complementarity ($x = 20$) are shown. As design B coincides with the non-hierarchical architecture it always follows $\Delta_m^{HSV} = 0$. Very small values $0.1 > \Delta_m^{HSV} > 0$ or $0 > \Delta_m^{HSV} > -0.1$ are denoted "< 0.1" and "> −0.1" respectively.

Table 6 shows the relative difference in value capture between the analyzed hierarchical bargaining structure and a non-hierarchical bargaining structure, Δ_m^{HSV}, for

Δ_m^{HSV} for essential firm E	Level of complementarity (x)	# of L1 clusters of firms: Minimum (2) — Number of firms (n): 3	10	100	10^6	Maximum — Number of firms (n): 3	10	100	10^6
E not clustered with any non-essential firm on L1 (A / B)	1.5	1.7	6.5	9.5	10.0	0	0	0	0
	2.0	3.7	12.0	16.2	16.7	0	0	0	0
	2.5	5.7	16.4	20.9	21.4	0	0	0	0
	3.0	7.4	19.8	24.5	25.0	0	0	0	0
	20	16.7	38.7	44.7	45.2	0	0	0	0
E clustered with 1 non-essential firm on L1 (C / D)	1.5	1.7	5.4	9.3	10.0	1.7	1.0	0.1	<0.1
	2.0	0.3	8.6	15.7	16.7	0.3	0.1	<0.1	<0.1
	2.5	-1.1	11.2	20.3	21.4	-1.1	-0.6	-0.1	>-0.1
	3.0	-2.4	13.3	23.8	25.0	-2.4	-1.2	-0.1	>-0.1
	20	-8.3	16.7	40.2	45.2	-8.3	-4.3	-0.4	>-0.1

E clustered with *n-2* non-essential firms on L1 (E)	Level of complementarity (x)	Number of firms (n): 3	10	100	10^6
	1.5	1.7	1.0	0.1	<0.1
	2.0	0.3	0.1	<0.1	<0.1
	2.5	-1.1	-0.6	-0.1	>-0.1
	3.0	-2.4	-1.2	-0.1	>-0.1
	20	-8.3	-4.3	-0.4	>-0.1

Table 6: Relative difference (Δ_m^{HSV}) between value appropriation in hierarchical and non-hierarchical bargaining structures for essential firm *E*

the essential firm *E*.[19] The results show that *E* has the highest relative value capture compared to the non-hierarchical structure in case A, in which *E* is not clustered with any non-essential firm and bargains with a single representative for all other firms. Given strict complementarity, the focal hierarchical bargaining structure (case A) allows *E* to appropriate a larger share of the overall value (often more than 10% if the

[19] Table 6 shows for each of the reference bargaining structures the relative difference in value capture of *E* for different sizes of bargaining structures ("Number of firms") and levels of complementarity. Note that all bargaining structures are strictly complementary because of $x > 1$. That is, the value created and to be distributed exponentially increases with the number of firms participating. A vertical comparison of cases, for example, comparing case A with case C or E, provides a perspective how the relative value capture changes with increasing number of firms clustered with the essential firm *E*. A horizontal comparison indicates the change in relative value capture if the overall number of L1 clusters is changed. For example, given a bargaining structure consisting of 100 firms and strict complementarity with $x = 2$, that is, $v(J) = |J|^2$ for $E \in J \subseteq M$, *E* captures in the hierarchical bargaining structure of case A 16.2% of the total value more than in the non-hierarchical bargaining structure. If a second non-essential firm is clustered with *E* (case C), it captures less value, in detail, 15.7% more than in the non-hierarchical bargaining structure. As the value capture of the total bargaining structure and the vale distribution in the non-hierarchical case are the same for both cases, one can conclude that *E* captures 0.5% less in case C than in case A.

bargaining structure involves more than 10 firms) than in a non-hierarchical setup. Further, keeping the number of firms clustered with E constant, the results suggest that increasing the overall number of clusters decreases the relative value capture of E. This statement will be analytically proofed in the latter part of this section. In addition, the fewer non-essential firms are clustered with the essential firm E the more favorable is a hierarchical bargaining structure for E with regard to value capture.

Further, the results in Table 7 show for the non-essential firm that is in a cluster with E that in cases with reasonable complementarity a non-hierarchical bargaining structure would be most beneficial. However, if the bargaining structure is hierarchical and the focal firm tied to the essential firm in a cluster, value appropriation increases with the number of firms that are as well included in the cluster and with a lower number of participants in top-level negotiation (that is, a lower number of clusters).

Conversely, other non-essential firms (outside the cluster containing E) can appropriate more value the more firms are clustered with E (see Table 8). Further, a bargaining structure is most beneficial for a non-essential firm if it directly participates in top-level negotiations (without being part of a larger cluster).

In total, given strict, exponentially increasing complementarity, every firm, regardless of its essential or non-essential character, benefits from being directly

Δ_m^{HSV} for non-essential firm clustered with E (on L1)	Level of complementarity (x)	# of L1 clusters of firms: Minimum (2) — Number of firms (n): 3	10	100	10^6	Maximum — Number of firms (n): 3	10	100	10^6
E not clustered with any non-essential firm on L1	(A)  / (B) 								
	1.5	n/a				n/a			
	2.0	n/a				n/a			
	2.5	n/a				n/a			
	3.0	n/a				n/a			
	20	n/a				n/a			
E clustered with 1 non-essential firm on L1	(C) 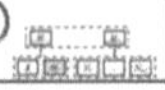 / (D) 								
	1.5	-3.5	-2.1	-0.2	>-0.1	-3.5	-2.5	-0.3	>-0.1
	2.0	-4.0	-1.9	-0.2	>-0.1	-4.0	-2.8	-0.3	>-0.1
	2.5	-4.5	-1.5	-0.1	>-0.1	-4.5	-3.0	-0.4	>-0.1
	3.0	-5.0	-0.9	>-0.1	>-0.1	-5.0	-3.2	-0.4	>-0.1
	20	-8.3	12.1	3.6	<0.1	-8.3	-4.3	-0.5	>-0.1

E clustered with n-2 non-essential firms on L1 (E) 	Level of complementarity (x)	Number of firms (n): 3	10	100	10^6
	1.5	-3.5	-0.3	>-0.1	>-0.1
	2.0	-4.0	-0.3	>-0.1	>-0.1
	2.5	-4.5	-0.4	>-0.1	>-0.1
	3.0	-5.0	-0.6	>-0.1	>-0.1
	20	-8.3	-3.7	-0.1	>-0.1

Table 7: Relative difference (Δ_m^{HSV}) between value appropriation in hierarchical and non-hierarchical bargaining structures for a non-essential firm being part of the same cluster as E

Δ_m^{HSV} **for non-essential firm not clustered with** ***E*** — **# of L1 clusters of firms**: **Minimum (2)** / **Maximum**

E **not clustered with any non-essential firm** on L1

Minimum (2): Ⓐ 

		Number of firms (n)			
		3	*10*	*100*	10^6
Level of complementarity (x)	*1.5*	-0.9	-0.7	-0.1	>-0.1
	2.0	-1.9	-1.3	-0.2	>-0.1
	2.5	-2.8	-1.8	-0.2	>-0.1
	3.0	-3.7	-2.2	-0.2	>-0.1
	20	-8.3	-4.3	-0.5	>-0.1

Maximum: Ⓑ 

		Number of firms (n)			
		3	*10*	*100*	10^6
Level of complementarity (x)	*1.5*	0	0	0	0
	2.0	0	0	0	0
	2.5	0	0	0	0
	3.0	0	0	0	0
	20	0	0	0	0

E clustered with **1 non-essential firm** on L1

Minimum (2): Ⓒ 

		Number of firms (n)			
		3	*10*	*100*	10^6
Level of complementarity (x)	*1.5*	1.7	-0.4	-0.1	>-0.1
	2.0	3.7	-0.8	-0.2	>-0.1
	2.5	5.6	-1.2	-0.2	>-0.1
	3.0	7.4	-1.5	-0.2	>-0.1
	20	16.7	-3,6	-0.4	>-0.1

Maximum: Ⓓ 

		Number of firms (n)			
		3	*10*	*100*	10^6
Level of complementarity (x)	*1.5*	1.7	0.2	<0.1	<0.1
	2.0	3.7	0.3	<0.1	<0.1
	2.5	5.7	0.5	<0.1	<0.1
	3.0	7.4	0.6	<0.1	<0.1
	20	16.7	1.1	<0.1	<0.1

E clustered with ***n-2*** **non-essential firms** on L1

Ⓔ 

		Number of firms (n)			
		3	*10*	*100*	10^6
Level of complementarity (x)	*1.5*	1.7	1.2	0.1	<0.1
	2.0	3.7	2.7	0.3	<0.1
	2.5	5.6	4.2	0.5	<0.1
	3.0	7.4	5.8	0.7	<0.1
	20	16.7	34.1	8.1	<0.1

Table 8: Relative difference (Δ_m^{HSV}) between value appropriation in hierarchical and non-hierarchical bargaining structures for a non-essential firm not being part of the same cluster as E

involved in top-level negotiations. Being part of a cluster of firms has a negative effect on value capture. The results are in line with Proposition 2 and Proposition 3 as most complementarity effects are realized on top-level (due to the bargaining structure in which the essential firm is mostly not clustered with many non-essential firms and the exponential characteristic function that creates increasing complementarity gains).

In the following, the statement that a stand-alone essential firm captures the more value the less clusters are created, that is, the more hierarchical the bargaining structure is generalized for bargaining structures with strict exponentially increasing complementarity. Therefore, I examine a hierarchical bargaining structure with an arbitrary number of clusters and a stand-alone essential firm involved in top-level negotiations, modify it through merging two non-essential clusters, and compare the corresponding value distributions.

Formally, let again be M the set of $n \in \mathbb{N}$ firms in the bargaining structure, let E denote the essential firm and N a non-essential firm. Let the $n-1$ non-essential firms be grouped in $k \in \mathbb{N}$ clusters (denoted by $M_1, \dots, M_k$) of equal size, each consisting of

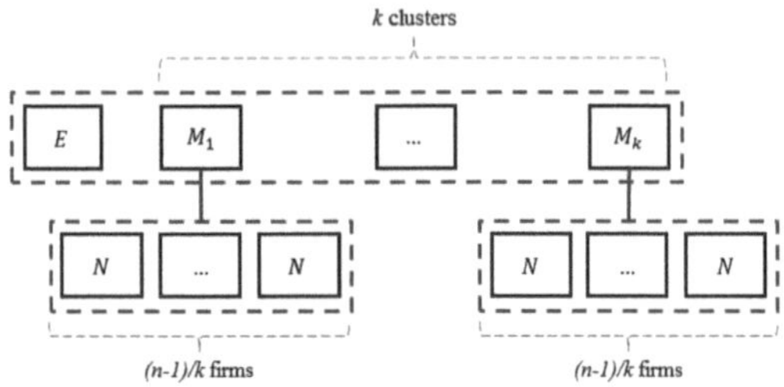

Figure 4: Illustration of bargaining structure with $\mathfrak{B} = \{E, M_1, \dots, M_k\}$

$(n-1)/k$ firms.[20] That is, a L1 bargaining structure $\mathfrak{B} = \{E, M_1, \dots M_k\}$ consisting of $k+1$ clusters including E is created (see Figure 4). Assuming again strict complementarity and using the characteristic function $v(J) = |J|^x$ for $J \subseteq M$ with $E \in J$ and $x > 1$, and $v(J) = 0$ for $J \subseteq M$ with $E \notin J$, the value appropriated by E in structure $\mathfrak{B}$ is determined by

$$\phi_E\,(\hat{v}, \mathfrak{B}) = \sum_{S \subseteq \mathfrak{B} \setminus \{E\}} \frac{|S|!\,(k-|S|)!}{(k+1)!} \big(\hat{v}(S \cup E) - \hat{v}(S)\big). \qquad (9)$$

As M_1 and M_2 will be merged in the latter bargaining structure the terms that are related to these clusters are separated from the rest:

$$\begin{aligned}\phi_E\,(\hat{v}, \mathfrak{B}) = &\sum_{S \subseteq \mathfrak{B} \setminus \{E, M_1, M_2\}} \frac{|S|!\,(k-|S|)!}{(k+1)!} \hat{v}(S \cup E) \\ &+ \sum_{\substack{S' \subseteq \mathfrak{B} \setminus \{E\}: \\ M_1 \in S' \wedge M_2 \notin S' \text{ or} \\ M_2 \in S' \wedge M_1 \notin S'}} \frac{|S'|!\,(k-|S'|)!}{(k+1)!} \hat{v}(S' \cup E) \\ &+ \sum_{\substack{S'' \subseteq \mathfrak{B} \setminus \{E\}: \\ M_1, M_2 \in S''}} \frac{|S''|!\,(k-|S''|)!}{(k+1)!} \hat{v}(S'' \cup E)\end{aligned}$$

Because of symmetry among non-essential firms and M_1 and M_2 are of equal size, the statement above is equal to:

---

20 Assuming that the number of non-essential firms $n-1$ is divisible by k, i.e., $(n-1)/k \in \mathbb{N}$.

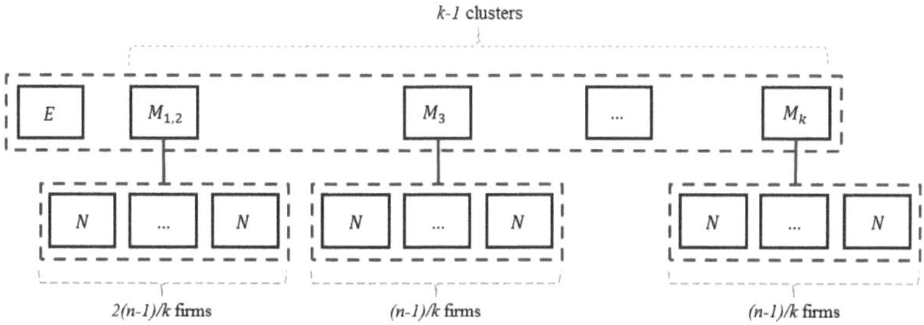

Figure 5: Illustration of bargaining structure with consolidated clusters M_1 and M_2, $\mathfrak{B}' = \{E, M_{1,2}, M_3, \dots, M_k\}$

$$\sum_{S \subseteq \mathfrak{B} \setminus \{E, M_1, M_2\}} \frac{|S|!\,(k-|S|)!}{(k+1)!} \hat{v}(S \cup E)$$

$$+2 \sum_{S \subseteq \mathfrak{B} \setminus \{E, M_1, M_2\}} \frac{(|S|+1)!\,(k-|S|-1)!}{(k+1)!} \hat{v}(S \cup E \cup M_1)$$

$$+ \sum_{S \subseteq \mathfrak{B} \setminus \{E, M_1, M_2\}} \frac{(|S|+2)!\,(k-|S|-2)!}{(k+1)!} \hat{v}(S \cup E \cup M_1 \cup M_2)$$

$$= \sum_{i=0}^{k-2} \binom{k-2}{i} \frac{1}{(k+1)!} \left[i!\,(k-i)! \left(\frac{n-1}{k} i + 1 \right)^x \right]$$

$$+2 \left[(i+1)!\,(k-i-1)! \left(\frac{n-1}{k} (i+1) + 1 \right)^x \right]$$

$$+ \left[(i+2)!\,(k-i-2)! \left(\frac{n-1}{k} (i+2) + 1 \right)^x \right]$$

For the second bargaining structure M_1 and M_2 are merged and a new cluster called $M_1 M_2$ consisting of $2(n-1)/k$ firms is created. Hence, the new bargaining structure $\mathfrak{B}' = \{E, M_{1,2}, M_3, \dots, M_k\}$ consists of k clusters (see Figure 5). The value capture of E is as follows:

$$\phi_E\,(\hat{v}, \mathfrak{B}') = \sum_{S \subseteq \mathfrak{B}' \setminus \{E\}} \frac{|S|!\,(k-|S|-1)!}{k!} \big(\hat{v}(S \cup E) - \hat{v}(S) \big)$$

$$= \sum_{S \subseteq \mathfrak{B}' \setminus \{E, M_{1,2}\}} \frac{|S|!\,(k-|S|-1)!}{k!} \hat{v}(S \cup E)$$

$$+\sum_{\substack{S'\subseteq\mathfrak{B}'\setminus\{E\}:\\ M_{1,2}\in S'}}\frac{|S'|!\,(k-|S'|-1)!}{k!}\hat{v}(S'\cup E)$$

$$=\sum_{S\subseteq\mathfrak{B}'\setminus\{E,M_{1,2}\}}\frac{|S|!\,(k-|S|-1)!}{k!}\hat{v}(S\cup E)$$

$$+\sum_{S\subseteq\mathfrak{B}'\setminus\{E,M_{1,2}\}}\frac{(|S|+1)!\,(k-|S|-2)!}{k!}\hat{v}\big(S\cup E\cup M_{1,2}\big)$$

$$=\sum_{i=0}^{k-2}\binom{k-2}{i}\frac{1}{k!}\left[i!\,(k-i-1)!\left(\frac{n-1}{k}i+1\right)^{x}\right]$$

$$+\left[(i+1)!\,(k-i-2)!\left(\frac{n-1}{k}(i+2)+1\right)^{x}\right]$$

To understand which bargaining structure is more favorable for E the difference between E's value capture in $\mathfrak{B}'$ and $\mathfrak{B}$ is now analyzed.

$$\phi_E\,(\hat{v},\mathfrak{B}')-\phi_E\,(\hat{v},\mathfrak{B})=\sum_{i=0}^{k-2}\binom{k-2}{i}\frac{(i+1)!\,(k-i-1)!}{(k+1)!}\times$$

$$\left[\left(\frac{n-1}{k}i+1\right)^{x}-2*\left(\frac{n-1}{k}(i+1)+1\right)^{x}+\left(\frac{n-1}{k}(i+2)+1\right)^{x}\right]$$

As the first part of every term of the sum is positive, I focus on the terms in the large bracket. With $y:=\frac{n-1}{k}$ and through applying the generalized binominal theorem twice for every summand in the bracket, it follows that

$$(yi+1)^x-2(y(i+1)+1)^x+(y(i+2)+1)^x$$

$$=\sum_{j=0}^{\infty}\binom{x}{j}(yi)^{x-j}-2\sum_{j=0}^{\infty}\binom{x}{j}(yi)^{x-j}(y+1)^j+\sum_{j=0}^{\infty}\binom{x}{j}(yi)^{x-j}(2y+1)^j$$

$$=\sum_{j=0}^{\infty}\binom{x}{j}(yi)^{x-j}\left[1-2(y+1)^j+(2y+1)^j\right]$$

$$=\sum_{j=0}^{\infty}\binom{x}{j}(yi)^{x-j}\left[1+\sum_{l=0}^{\infty}\binom{j}{l}2^ly^l-2y^l\right]>0\;\forall i\;and\;x>1.$$

Hence, $\phi_E\ (\hat{v}, \mathfrak{B}') - \phi_E\ (\hat{v}, \mathfrak{B}) > 0$ holds, that is the value capture of E is higher in a bargaining structure with a consolidated clusters $M_{1,2}$ than in the one with separate clusters M_1 and M_2.

This setup mirrors the situation of a strong OEM in a value chain consisting of more or less replaceable suppliers. OEMs are in many cases hard to replace in the value chain not only because of their integration capabilities (which may be trivial) but because of their brand and customer access. In cases in which none of the suppliers is in a bottleneck position, neither providing critical inputs to the value chain nor is in a monopoly-like situation in its component market, the OEM can increase its value capture through a consolidation of the supplier landscape. This leads to the following proposition:

PROPOSITION 4: *In value chains with strong, non-replaceable OEMs, non-essential suppliers, and exponentially increasing complementarity, the OEM can enhance value capture through consolidating direct suppliers, hence increasing the level of hierarchy of the bargaining structure.*

In order to further generalize the result, I will now evaluate the case without any essential firms and without a specific characteristic function. In particular, I drop the assumption of increasing complementarity. Let F be the stand-alone firm (analogue to E in the case discussed above) and $M_1, \dots M_k$, $k \in \mathbb{N}$ the L1-clusters of firms. Note that, for the moment, the number of firms in each cluster is not specified. Again, I compare the value capture between the bargaining structures $\mathfrak{B} = \{F, M_1, \dots, M_k\}$ and $\mathfrak{B}' = \{F, M_{1,2}, \dots, M_k\}$ in which two clusters are merged. According to the HSV, value capture of F in $\mathfrak{B}$ is

$$\phi_F\ (\hat{v}, \mathfrak{B}) = \sum_{S \subseteq \mathfrak{B} \setminus \{F, M_1, M_2\}} \frac{|S|!\,(k - |S|)!}{(k+1)!} \big(\hat{v}(S \cup F) - \hat{v}(S)\big)$$

$$+ \sum_{S \subseteq \mathfrak{B} \setminus \{F, M_1, M_2\}} \frac{(|S|+1)!\,(k - |S| - 1)!}{(k+1)!} \big(\hat{v}(S \cup F \cup M_1) - \hat{v}(S \cup M_1)$$

$$+ \hat{v}(S \cup F \cup M_2) - \hat{v}(S \cup M_2)\big)$$

$$+ \sum_{S \subseteq \mathfrak{B} \setminus \{F, M_1, M_2\}} \frac{(|S|+2)!\,(k - |S| - 2)!}{(k+1)!} \big(\hat{v}(S \cup F \cup M_1 \cup M_2)$$

$$- \hat{v}(S \cup M_1 \cup M_2)\big).$$

Similarly, the value capture of F in $\mathfrak{B}'$ is

$$\phi_F(\hat{v},\mathfrak{B}') = \sum_{S\subseteq\mathfrak{B}'\setminus\{F,M_{1,2}\}} \frac{|S|!\,(k-|S|-1)!}{k!}\big(\hat{v}(S\cup F)-\hat{v}(S)\big)$$
$$+\sum_{S\subseteq\mathfrak{B}'\setminus\{F,M_{1,2}\}} \frac{(|S|+1)!\,(k-|S|-2)!}{k!}\Big(\hat{v}\big(S\cup F\cup M_{1,2}\big)-\hat{v}\big(S\cup M_{1,2}\big)\Big).$$

Consequently, the consolidation of clusters is beneficial for F if $\phi_F(\hat{v},\mathfrak{B}') - \phi_F(\hat{v},\mathfrak{B}) > 0$, that is, if

$$\sum_{S\subseteq\mathfrak{B}'\setminus\{F,M_{1,2}\}} \left(\frac{|S|!\,(k-|S|-1)!}{k!}-\frac{|S|!\,(k-|S|)!}{(k+1)!}\right)\big(\hat{v}(S\cup F)-\hat{v}(S)\big)$$
$$+\sum_{S\subseteq\mathfrak{B}'\setminus\{F,M_{1,2},\}} \left(\frac{(|S|+1)!\,(k-|S|-2)!}{k!}-\frac{(|S|+2)!\,(k-|S|-2)!}{(k+1)!}\right)\times$$
$$\Big(\hat{v}\big(S\cup F\cup M_{1,2}\big)-\hat{v}\big(S\cup M_{1,2}\big)\Big)$$
$$-\sum_{S\subseteq\mathfrak{B}'\setminus\{F,M_{1,2}\}} \frac{(|S|+1)!\,(k-|S|-1)!}{(k+1)!}\big(\hat{v}(S\cup F\cup M_1)-\hat{v}(S\cup M_1)$$
$$+\hat{v}(S\cup F\cup M_2)-\hat{v}(S\cup M_2)\big)$$
$$=\sum_{S\subseteq\mathfrak{B}'\setminus\{F,M_{1,2}\}} \frac{(|S|+1)!\,(k-|S|-1)!}{(k+1)!}\Big(\hat{v}(S\cup F)-\hat{v}(S)+\hat{v}\big(S\cup F\cup M_{1,2}\big)$$
$$-\hat{v}\big(S\cup M_{1,2}\big)-\hat{v}(S\cup F\cup M_1)+\hat{v}(S\cup M_1)-\hat{v}(S\cup F\cup M_2)$$
$$+\hat{v}(S\cup M_2)\Big)$$
$$>0.$$

Through using the complementary gains $\Delta_{J,F} := \hat{v}(J\cup F)-\hat{v}(S)-\hat{v}(F)$ for $J\subseteq \mathfrak{B}\setminus F$ the focal firm F benefits from a consolidation of clusters if

$$\sum_{S\subseteq\mathfrak{B}'\setminus\{F,M_{1,2}\}} \frac{(|S|+1)!\,(k-|S|-1)!}{(k+1)!}\big(\Delta_{S,F}+\Delta_{(S\cup M_{1,2}),F}$$
$$-\Delta_{(S\cup M_1),F}-\Delta_{(S\cup M_2),F}\big)>0. \tag{10}$$

PROPOSITION 5: *A consolidation of two L1 clusters is beneficial for a stand-alone firm F with a position in top-level negotiations if inequality* (10) *holds. This is true in particular if complementarity between the focal firm and the merged clusters is larger than the sum of complementarities in the unconsolidated case given the presence of an arbitrary group of firms (excluding F and the focal clusters).*

The weights of the complementarity gains in inequality (10) are particularly high for summands in which either no firms or all other firms are present. The sum of weights for $|S| = 0$ and $|S| = k - 2$ is in relation to the sum of weights of all other summands in inequality (10) larger than $\frac{k-1}{k-3} > 1$. Hence, a consolidation of the focal clusters is most likely beneficial for the stand-alone firm F if for these two summands (that is, where either no other firms are present or the value chain is complete) complementarity between F and the merged clusters is larger than the sum of complementarities in the unconsolidated case.

4.2.3 Multiple bargaining positions

In this section, the assumption that a firm participates only once in the bargaining structure is relaxed. That is, I analyze the value capture of a firm occupying several positions in the bargaining structure. A firm can have positions in different independent negotiations (for example, being an upstream seller and a downstream buyer of the unfinished product, or a seller of components to different upstream firms), or several positions within a single negotiation.[21] Two bargaining positions of a firm are called "connected" if they are part of the same negotiation, if they are on different hierarchical levels but in the same branch of negotiations in the tree-like bargaining structure,[22] or if there is a third position of the focal firm in a higher level negotiation that can be seen as the root of the lower-level negotiations in the tree-like bargaining structure. See Figure 6 for illustrations of connected and unconnected positions.

Having connected positions might provide the option to consolidate them and capture the value of the consolidated position.[23] Alternatively, a firm has the option to

---

[21] A firm may contribute different products that are managed by separate entities (for example, subsidiaries or business units) to a value chain. Thus, a firm can have several positions in a negotiation.

[22] For example, if a firm owns positions in top-level negotiation and in L2 negotiations of an unrelated cluster.

[23] Note that a firm with several positions may not be able to consolidate them. For example, being a tier-2 producer to different tier-1 suppliers does not allow consolidation the positions.

capture the value of each of its positions independently. If connected positions would naturally result in a consolidated position, I assume the firm has the option to split them by selling one of them (with the corresponding assets) to a third party for a fair price.

The case of a single firm in the value chain having two positions in the bargaining structure serves as a starting point to derive first insights. Without loss of generality, let m_1 and m_3 be the positions of the focal firm. Formally, for the consolidated case the set of bargaining positions $M = \{m_1, \dots, m_N\}$, $N \in \mathbb{N}$ is reduced to $M^* = \{m_{1,3}, m_2 m_4,, \dots m_n\}$. [24] Using the characteristic function $v: 2^M \to \mathbb{R}$ on M a characteristic function $v^*: 2^{M^*} \to \mathbb{R}$ on M^* is defined as $v^*(m_{1,3} \cup J) := v(m_1 \cup m_3 \cup J)$ and $v^*(J) := v(J)$ for $J \subseteq M^* \backslash \{m_{1,3}\}$.

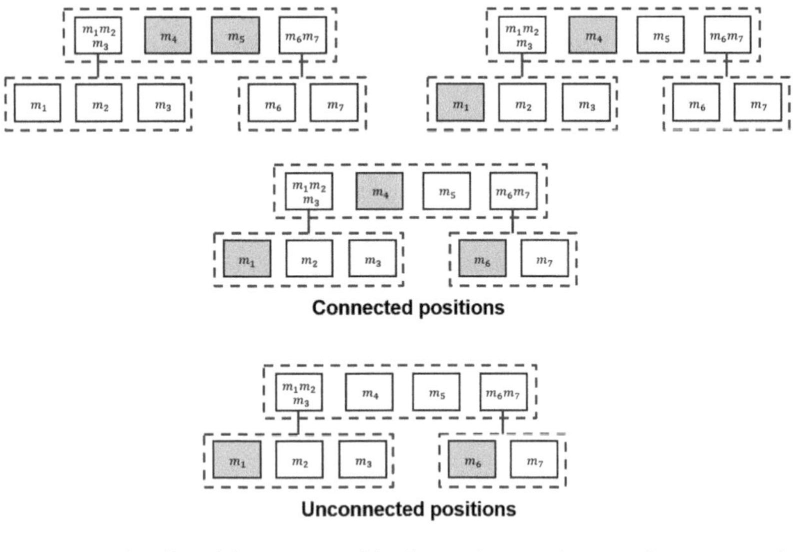

Figure 6: Examples of bargaining structures with a firm owning several connected or unconnected positions

[24] Note that M refers no longer to the firms participating in the bargaining structure but to all bargaining positions. In the preceding sections, every firm owned exactly one position, thus, the set of bargaining firms and positions coincided.

Starting with the basic non-hierarchical three-firm bargaining structure with $M = \{m_1, m_2, m_3\}$ that is reduced to the two-firm bargaining structure with $M^* = \{m_{1,3}, m_2\}$ keeping the bargaining positions m_1 and m_3 separate is beneficial if

$$\begin{aligned}&\phi_{m_1}(v) + \phi_{m_3}(v) > \phi_{m_{1,3}}(v^*)\\ &\Leftrightarrow \big(v(m_1) + v(m_2) + v(m_3)\big) - \big(v(m_1 m_2) + v(m_1 m_3) + v(m_2 m_3)\big)\\ &\qquad\qquad + v(m_1 m_2 m_3) > 0.\end{aligned}$$

Using complementarity gains, $\phi_{m_1}(v) + \phi_{m_3}(v) > \phi_{m_{1,3}}(v^*)$ holds if

$$\begin{aligned}&\Delta_{m_1,m_3} + \Delta_{m_2,m_3} + 2\Delta_{m_1,(m_2 m_3)} + 2\Delta_{m_2,(m_1 m_3)}\\ &\qquad > 4\Delta_{m_1,m_2} + 3\Delta_{(m_1 m_2),m_3}.\end{aligned} \tag{11}$$

Consequently, if both positions m_1 and m_3 are essential, keeping them separate is beneficial if $v(M) > v(m_1 m_3)$. Hence, if there is complementarity among all positions, keeping them separate is beneficial, or at least indifferent. Conversely, consolidating essential positions hurts value capture. Similarly, if one of the bargaining positions m_1, m_2 is essential and m_3 is essential, splitting positions is always beneficial. In other cases, splitting (or keeping positions separate) tends to be advantageous in value chains with strongly increasing complementarity (which is not always the case)[25], that is if complementarity between any two positions is relatively low compared to the complementarity created among all three firms.

Applying the characteristic function defined according to Table 1 with $0 < \alpha \leq \beta \leq 1$ (assuming symmetry of non-essential firms), the results (see Table 9) illustrate the discussed findings. In the non-hierarchical case, if there are more than two essential positions, splitting positions is beneficial for the focal firm. Further, splitting is beneficial if complementarity between the two positions is relatively low, in concrete terms, if the value add of the second position is smaller than a third of the overall value in the case of no essential positions, and if complementarity between the positions is

---

[25] For example, the wireless technologies NFC and Bluetooth for smartphones are not complementary as they have overlapping use cases. However, both can be found in smartphones at the same time.

Number of essential positions in M		Splitting position
m_1, m_3	m_2	$m_{1,3}$ is beneficial if
0	0	$\beta - \alpha < \frac{1}{3}$
1	0	$\beta - \alpha < 1 - \beta$
0	1	$\beta - \alpha < 1 - \beta$
2	0	$\beta < 1$, that is always
1	1	$\beta < 1$, that is always
2	1	$\frac{1}{2} < \frac{2}{3}$, that is always

Table 9: Splitting positions in a non-hierarchical three-firm bargaining structure

smaller than complementarity on top-level in the case of one essential position (m_1 or m_3).

In hierarchical bargaining structures, I analyze the option to merge a position within a cluster with another position of the focal firm in top-level bargaining. In the three-firm bargaining structure (see Figure 7), a firm having positions m_1 and m_3 has the option to keep the bargaining structure as is, or consolidate its positions into a single position $m_{1,3}$. This would change the set of bargaining positions to $M^* = \{m_{1,3}, m_2\}$ and result in a non-hierarchical bargaining structure. Splitting positions (or keeping the positions separated) is beneficial for the firm owning positions m_1 and m_3 if the sum of value

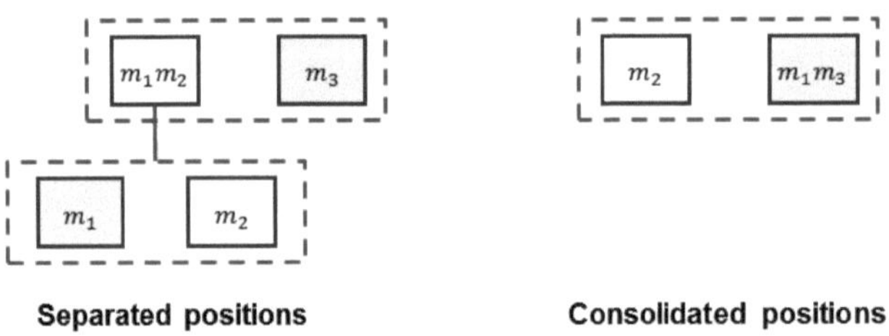

Figure 7: Consolidating or splitting positions in a three-firm hierarchical bargaining structure

capture in the unconsolidated case exceeds the value capture in the consolidated case, that is, if $\phi_{m_1}^{HSV}(v,\mathfrak{B}) + \phi_{m_3}^{HSV}(v,\mathfrak{B}) > \phi_{m_{13}}(v^*)$. This is equal to

$$\frac{v(m_1m_2)(v(m_1m_3) - v(m_2m_3))}{v(m_1m_2m_3) - v(m_3)} + 2v(m_2) + v(m_3) - v(m_1m_2) - v(m_1m_3) - v(m_2m_3) + v(m_1m_2m_3) > 0.$$

Using complementarity gains, the above statement can be modified to

$$\Delta_{(m_1m_3),m_2} - \Delta_{m_1,m_2} - \Delta_{m_2,m_3} + \frac{v(m_1m_2)(v(m_1m_3) - v(m_2m_3))}{v(m_1m_2m_3) - v(m_3)} - v(m_1) + v(m_2) > 0. \quad (12)$$

Inequality (12) shows that similarly to the non-hierarchical case splitting is always beneficial if both positions of the focal firm are essential (since only $\Delta_{(m_1m_3),m_2} \neq 0$).

Likewise, assuming symmetry of non-essential firms and applying the characteristic function defined according to Table 1 with $0 < \alpha \leq \beta \leq 1$, the results (see Table 10) show that splitting is beneficial if there are more than two essential firms in the

Essential positions in *M*	**Splitting position $\boldsymbol{m_{1,3}}$ is beneficial if**
-	$\beta - \alpha < \frac{1}{3}$
m_1	$\beta < \frac{1}{2}$
m_2	$\beta - \alpha < \frac{1}{2}$
m_3	$\beta - \alpha < 1 - \beta$
m_1, m_2	$\beta < 1$, that is always
m_2, m_3	$\beta < 1$, that is always
m_1, m_3	$\beta < 1$, that is always
m_1, m_2, m_3	$0 < 1$, that is always

Table 10: Splitting positions in a hierarchical three-firm bargaining structure

bargaining structure. Further, if complementarity between individual positions is low (and consequently complementarity in completing the value chain is rather high if the characteristic function is strongly increasing with number of firms involved), splitting tends to be beneficial.

All in all, the results suggest the following proposition:

PROPOSITION 6: *A firm owning several positions in a given bargaining structure may have the option to consolidate or split its positions to increase value capture. Splitting positions is beneficial for a firm owning two positions in a non-hierarchical three-firm bargaining structure if inequality (11) holds; in a hierarchical three-firm bargaining structure if inequality (12) holds. Thus, if both positions of the focal firm are essential splitting is in most cases beneficial. In return, integrating essential positions decreases value capture. In case of symmetry among non-essential firms, splitting is advantageous if there are two or more essential positions in the bargaining structure, or if complementarity among individual positions is relatively small (which implies that complementarity created among all positions involved is rather high in bargaining structures with increasing complementarities towards the top-level).*

As the results show, in particular in value chains with increasing complementarity firms can benefit from splitting their positions in the bargaining structure (if possible). However, relaxing the assumption of fixed total, too many bargaining positions can lead to an underuse of the production capacity of the value chain and a decrease of value creation, especially if all have the power to create a holdup—a situation known as the tragedy of anti-commons (Heller and Eisenberg 1998).

4.3 Extensions and further results

The following sections extend the introduced model by two important aspects to better represent realistic value chains and bargaining structures. First, up to now I have assumed that system integration capabilities are available in competitive supply and hence, that the integrator, who may represent the cluster in top-level negotiations, does not appropriate any rent. However, in many cases the system integrator is costly to replace and, thus, has a powerful role in the value chain. Therefore, in Section 4.3.1 the effect of integrators on value distribution will be modeled and analyzed. Second, firms facing (nearly) perfect competition do not capture any value, although they are part of the value chain and contribute to value creation. Practically, this is the case for commodity goods manufacturers. Similarly, open source contributors enhance value creation without directly appropriating any value. In Section 4.3.2 it will be evaluated who benefits most from non-value-appropriating players.

4.3.1 System integrators

System integrators assemble components from suppliers to form the final product or subsystem. If integration is complex, integrators have a powerful role in the value chain as they are often difficult to replace (Jacobides and MacDuffie 2013) and essential to realize complementarity among firms. There are different roles that system integrators can take on. For example, many automotive OEMs and tier-1 suppliers are component/subsystem suppliers as well as system integrators and play central roles in the value chain and bargaining structure as they deliver the integrated product to the next upstream level (customer or OEM, respectively). On the other hand, the electronics device manufacturer Foxconn can be considered a pure integration service provider, being relatively easily to replace, with a similar role as a non-central component supplier in the bargaining structure. If system integration is critical, it is likely that the system integrator is the central firm that represents a cluster in the next higher level of the bargaining structure.

Integrators can be found on every level of the value chain, and if the value chain architecture and bargaining structure more or less coincide, they are on the top-level as well as within every cluster of a hierarchical bargaining structure.[26] Let $M_{int} := \left\{m_{int(L1)}, \left\{m_{int(M_i)}\right\}_{i=1,\ldots,k}\right\} \subseteq M$ be the set of essential integrators[27] on the top-level and within every cluster of firms M_i if the bargaining structure mirrors the value chain

[26] In case of a simple integration process the integrator might not be part of the bargaining structure although being part of the value chain. This case will be discussed in more detail in section 4.3.2.

[27] Note that the present model of the role of system integrator in the bargaining structure is confined to essential system integrators. A continuous parameterization of the replaceability of integrators is possible and, therefore, omitted in the present work.

architecture.[28] The integrators enable complementarity among the firms in the value chain. Without them, the value of the value chain would be only the sum of values obtained by individual component suppliers.

Starting from a value chain M without the need for integration services[29] with the relevant characteristic function $v: 2^M \rightarrow \mathbb{R}$, an induced function v^{int} on $M \cup M_{int}$ is defined with

$$v^{int}(J) := \begin{cases} v\left(\bigcup_{i:\, m_{int(M_i)} \in J} \bigcup_{m_j \in J \cap M_i} m_j\right) + \sum_{i:\, m_{int(M_i)} \notin J} \left(\sum_{m_j \in J \cap M_i} v(m_j)\right) & \text{if } m_{int(L1)} \in J \\ \sum_{i:\, m_{int(M_i)} \in J} v\left(\bigcup_{m_j \in J \cap M_i} m_j\right) + \sum_{i:\, m_{int(M_i)} \notin J} \left(\sum_{m_j \in J \cap M_i} v(m_j)\right) & \text{if } m_{int(L1)} \notin J \end{cases} \tag{13}$$

The definition implies that pure integrators do not have a stand-alone value, that is, the value without any other firm being present $v^{int}(K) = 0$ for $K \subseteq M_{int}$. Assuming that the integrators are essential (with regard to the integration function) it follows directly that thc top-level integrator appropriates a positive value if it enables complementarity among the clusters. Note that the definition of v^{int} coincides with a special case of the Myerson Value (Myerson 1977), which applies the SV concept to a non-hierarchical bargaining structure with a preset cooperation structure.

As several induced characteristic functions may be required at the same time for evaluating value capture, for example, $\check{v}_{M_i}$, for value distribution within a cluster M_i, and v^{int}, I define the following sequence for application of (induced) characteristic functions. The induced characteristic function v^{int} is the last characteristic function to be applied when solving an equation, that is, $v^{int} \circ \check{v}_{M_i}$ is applied, for example.

---

[28] Note that in the case of a non-hierarchical bargaining structure with a hierarchical value chain architecture having several integrators, $m_{int(M_i)}$ refers to the integration of firms that would form a cluster M_i if the bargaining structure would coincide with the value chain architecture.

[29] In the case of a system without the need for integration services, pure integrators are dummy players having neither a stand-alone value nor added value to any coalition of firms.

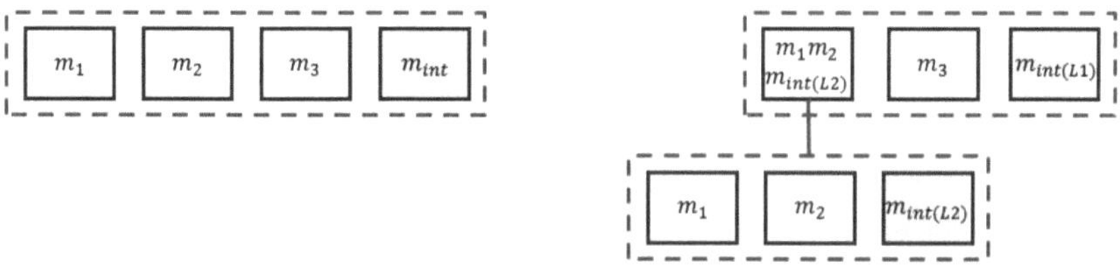

Figure 8: Illustration of non-hierarchical and hierarchical three-firm bargaining structures extended by integrators

Besides the integrator, the architect of the value chain (or parts thereof) has a similar role. In some cases, like in house construction projects, the architect is a separate firm, in many other cases it coincides with the role of the integrator or component supplier. Although the modeling of an architect would be analogous,[30] I will not explicitly include it in the further model. Further, note that the idea of a system integrator can be applied to bilateral bargaining situations in which a central firm bargains with the providers of inputs, which have little transparency of other participants and their value add. The central firm, that is not necessarily the firm performing the product-related integration activity, could be seen as the firm connecting all participants, thus, also being a sort of integrator.

To understand the value capture of system integrators and its effect on other firms in the bargaining structure, the basic example of three non-essential firms extended by pure system integrators is analyzed.

First, the new non-hierarchical bargaining structure consists of, besides m_1, m_2, m_3, an essential integrator firm m_{int}, which performs the full integration (see Figure 8). Using an arbitrary characteristic function $v: 2^M \to \mathbb{R}$ and the induced characteristic function $v^{int}: 2^{M \cup \{m_{int}\}} \to \mathbb{R}$ (according to Equation (13)) the integrator captures in the non-hierarchical bargaining structure $\phi_{m_{int}}(v^{int}) = \frac{1}{12}\left(\Delta_{m_1,m_2} + \Delta_{m_1,m_3} + \Delta_{m_2,m_3}\right) + \frac{1}{4}\Delta_{m_1,m_2,m_3}$.[31] That is, the integrator can appropriate a share of the complementarity

30 Complementarity would be realized only if integrator and architect are both present in the focal part of the bargaining structure.

31 Note that the complementarity gains $\Delta_{J,K}$ and $\Delta_{J,K,L}$ take the presence of the respective integrators as given (so that complementarity is indeed created). In the earlier definition of complementarity

created among all firms as well as among all pairs of firms, which equals about ¼ of the overall complementarity.

Second, in the hierarchical case the three-firm bargaining structure is extended by integrators both on the top-level and within the cluster, each performing the respective integration activity on its level. That is, $\mathfrak{B} = \left\{\{m_1, m_2, m_{int(L2)}\}, m_3, m_{int(L1)}\right\}$.[32] According to HSV, the top-level integrator $m_{int(L1)}$ captures a third of the top-level complementarity, that is,

$$\phi_{m_{int(L1)}}(v^{int} \circ \hat{v}, \mathfrak{B}) = \frac{1}{3}\Delta_{(m_1 \cup m_2),m_3}.$$

Further, the integrator of the cluster $m_{int(L2)}$ appropriates

$$\phi^{HSV}_{m_{int(L2)}}\left(v \circ \check{v}_{m_1 m_2 m_{int(L2)}}\right)$$

$$= \frac{v\left(m_1 m_2 m_{int(L2)}\right) + \frac{1}{3}\Delta_{(m_1 \cup m_2),m_3}}{3\left(v(M) - v(m_3)\right)} \left[\frac{1}{2}\left(\Delta_{m_1,m_3} + \Delta_{m_2,m_3}\right) + \Delta_{m_1,m_2,m_3}\right].$$

One can see that the sum of value appropriated by the integrators in the hierarchical case can exceed value capture in the non-hierarchical case. Using the characteristic function defined according to Table 1 with $0 < \alpha \leq \beta \leq 1$ (assuming symmetry of non-essential firms), the sum of value appropriated by the integrators can exceed the value appropriated in the non-hierarchical bargaining structure if $\alpha < 5/35$ and $(5 - 5\alpha)/8 < \beta < 1 - 5\alpha$. This means that a system integrator having sufficient capabilities is better off in a hierarchical bargaining structure being involved twice on different levels if there is strong complementarity involved.

gains, integrators were not explicitly considered. However, it was assumed that either integration is a trivial activity and can be performed by every firm or that the integration services are in competitive supply.

32 There is no need to introduce an integrator for the second cluster consisting only of m_3. As no integration is required for the trivial m_3 cluster, the integrator would be a dummy player and not appropriate any value.

Further, although m_3 captures less value than in a case without required system integrators (just as m_1 and m_2),[33] hierarchy remains beneficial for m_3 if $\Delta_{(m_1 \cup m_2),m_3} - \Delta_{m_1,m_3} - \Delta_{m_2 m_3} > 0$. Hence, the rule for deciding whether the hierarchical bargaining structure is advantageous holds regardless of the presence of pure system integrators. Consequently, Proposition 2 is extended.

PROPOSITION 7: *Being the single L1 firm in a hierarchical three-firm bargaining structure with additional essential system integrators on both levels is superior to being in a non-hierarchical bargaining structure (including a single system integrator) if and only if the focal firm's top-level complementarity gains $\Delta_{(m_1 \cup m_2),m_3}$ exceed the sum of possible cluster complementarity gains.*

Consequently, if hierarchy is beneficial for the stand-alone L1 firm m_3, then hierarchy is disadvantageous for the cluster $m_1 m_2$.

Further, the case studies in Section 5 will show that changes in the bargaining structure often go along with a new distribution of the integration activities. Therefore, in the following an example is discussed in which an essential integrator, presumably the OEM, delegates the integration of a part of the product to a tier-1 supplier.

A bargaining structure consisting of five firms, one of them being an essential firm m_{int} that is integrator and component supplier at the same time, will be analyzed. Hence, it is assumed that the stand-alone value $v(m_{int}) > 0$. The other firms are denoted with $m_1, \dots, m_4$. In the hierarchical bargaining structure m_1 takes over the integrator role for the cluster $M_{123} = \{m_1, m_2, m_3\}$. Thus, the hierarchical bargaining structure is given by $\mathfrak{B} = \{m_{int}, \{m_1, m_2, m_3\}, m_4\}$ (see Figure 9 for an illustration of the bargaining structures). I assume that m_{int} retains the capabilities for the integration activities. Therefore m_1 is easily replaceable in its integrator role and its stand-alone value does not change. Further, m_{int} stays essential due to its component supplier and integrator role on top-level.

---

33 In the non-hierarchical case, m_3 captures $\frac{1}{12}\left(\Delta_{m_1,m_3} + \Delta_{m_2,m_3} + \Delta_{(m_1 \cup m_2),m_3}\right)$ less if there is the need of system integrators; in the hierarchical bargaining structure, m_3 captures $\frac{1}{6}\Delta_{(m_1 \cup m_2),m_3}$ less.

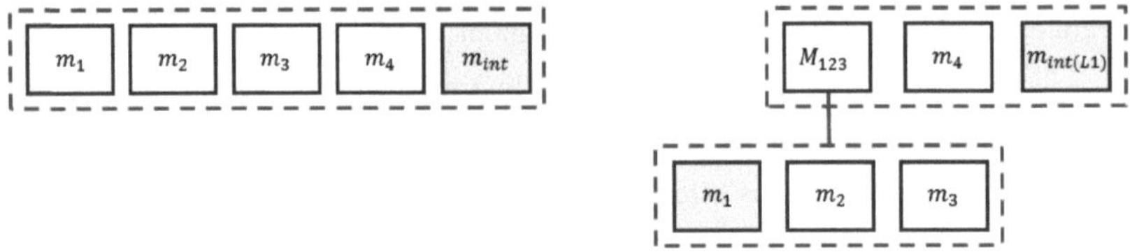

Figure 9: Illustration of the non-hierarchical and hierarchical bargaining structures with top-level integrators m_{int} and cluster integrator m_1

The characteristic function v in the hypothetical case that integration is not required, which is defined according to Table 11 with $0 < \alpha \leq \beta \leq \gamma \leq \delta \leq 1$, is used to derive the induced characteristic function v^{int}.

In the non-hierarchical bargaining structure m_{int} captures according to the SV $\phi_{m_{int}}(v^{int}) = \frac{1}{5}(1 + \alpha + \beta + \gamma + \delta)$ while all other firms capture $\phi_{m_1}(v^{int}) =\ldots= \phi_{m_4}(v^{int}) = \frac{1}{20}(4 - \alpha - \beta - \gamma - \delta)$.

$J \subseteq M$	$v(J)$
m_{int}	α
$m_i m_{int}\ for\ i \in \{1,2,3,4\}$	β
$m_i m_j m_{int}\ for\ i,j \in \{1,2,3,4\}, i \neq j$	γ
$m_i m_j m_k m_{int}\ for\ i,j,k \in \{1,2,3,4\}, i \neq j$	δ
$m_1 m_2 m_3 m_4 m_{int}$	1
Others	0

Table 11: Characteristic function $\boldsymbol{v}$ in the hypothetical case of integration services not being required

In the hierarchical bargaining structure, in which m_{int} only fulfills the integration on top-level, m_{int} captures $\frac{1}{3}(1 + \alpha + \frac{1}{2}(\beta + \delta))$. There are two opposing effects for m_{int} that come into play in the hierarchical bargaining structure. On the one side, m_{int} benefits from the consolidation of non-essential suppliers as it was shown in Proposition

4. On the other side, m_{int} has handed over some part of its integrator role and only fulfills the integration on top-level. However, the results show that m_{int} benefits from the new hierarchical structure if

$$\frac{1}{2}(\beta+\delta)+3\gamma<2+2\alpha, \tag{14}$$

that is, in particular if complementary effects are mostly realized in the final integration steps (i.e., $1-\delta$ and $1-\beta$ large or δ and β small) or m_{int} has a large stand-alone value (α large).

The same effects affect m_1 in the opposite direction. The integrator role brings additional value but at the same time the consolidation is disadvantageous. In the hierarchical bargaining structure m_1 can capture $\frac{1}{18(1-\beta)}(2-6\beta+2\gamma+2\delta+2)(1-\beta+\frac{1}{2}(\delta-\alpha))$. Thus, m_1 benefits if

$$\begin{aligned}16+\alpha+35\beta-29\gamma-39\delta+9\beta(\alpha+\beta+\gamma+\delta)\\+20\left(\beta-\frac{1}{2}(\delta-\alpha)\right)(-3\beta+\gamma+\delta)<0.\end{aligned} \tag{15}$$

As expected, this particularly holds if most complementarity effects are realized already before the integration on top-level (i.e., γ and δ large).

Further, the firms m_2 and m_3 lose from the new hierarchical bargaining structure if

$$\begin{aligned}70+18\beta(\alpha+\beta)+17\beta(\gamma+\delta)+\frac{1}{2}(\delta+\gamma)(\delta-\alpha)\\>18\delta+17\gamma+88\beta+17\alpha\end{aligned} \tag{16}$$

Among others, the inequality holds for all characteristic functions with $\beta<1/3$, as it follows that $70>18\delta+17\gamma+88\beta+17\alpha$. Hence, if there high complementarity gains can be realized in the final completion steps of the bargaining structure (thus β being small) m_2 and m_3 lose from their position in the cluster.

Nevertheless, in value chains with a low level of complementarity or in which complementarity is mostly realized among a small group of firms (i.e., α and β relatively large), a hierarchical bargaining structure might be in favor of the firms that are placed on a lower level of the bargaining structure.

PROPOSITION 8: *Given a non-hierarchical bargaining structure consisting of an essential integrator and four symmetric non-essential firms. If the top-level integrator creates a hierarchical bargaining structure by forming a cluster of three non-essential firms and handing over the integration to one of the participants of the cluster, the integrator can increase value capture if inequality (14) holds, that is, in particular, if most complementarity involved is realized on top-level. Conversely, if almost all complementarity is realized within clusters and, thus, inequality (15) holds while inequality (16) is violated, all firms in the cluster, including the integrator, benefit from the new hierarchical bargaining structure.*

Note that, as mentioned before, the concept of "essentiality" is the continuous extension and extreme case of a firm being "hard to replace". Therefore, the analyses that use the extreme case of essentiality to flesh out the results, can be seen as indications for the settings in which firms are nearly essential.

4.3.2 Free value

In the last sections, I developed a model that shows how value is split among the participants of a value chain and bargaining structure. However, there might be firms or individuals that are part of the value chain but not part of the bargaining structure—providing value to the system but not appropriating any. They are called in the following non-value-appropriating (NVA) firms. There are two factors an NVA character can be based on: perfect competition and open source components. First, firms facing perfect competition, for example, suppliers of commodities such as standardized screws or simple and commonly known integration processes, can be replaced easily and have no bargaining power. Therefore, the transfer of goods most likely will not be subject to negotiations and the focal firm will not be part of the bargaining structure. However, they increase the overall value available to the value chain. Similarly, developers of open source software freely provide all relevant product-related information (i.e., the software source code) and a license free of charge that allows others to copy, modify, or further develop the product (Open Source Initiative 2014). Thus, an open source component adds value without the respective developers appropriating any.

Note that there is a difference between non-essential and NVA firms. Perfect competition is the extreme case of being easily replaceable and non-essentiality; however, non-essential firms are part of the bargaining structure, thus, negotiating over their value capture, which is larger than zero. In contrast, NVA firms do not participate in the bargaining structure and do not appropriate any value.

The question arises as to which firms can appropriate the free value contributed by NVA firms. Firms in the bargaining structure that are aware of the presence of an NVA firm will try to benefit and incorporate the offering of the NVA firm in their propositions. However, only if the required integration capabilities are available they can, in fact, leverage the value of the NVA firm.

In a non-hierarchical bargaining structure I assume that all firms have transparency about other firms in the value chain. Hence, they are aware of the NVA firm m_{NVA} and attempt to benefit from it. Formally, if m_{NVA} was *not* NVA, then let $v'': 2^{M \cup m_{NVA}} \rightarrow \mathbb{R}$ be the relevant characteristic function on the set $M \cup m_{NVA}$. As a consequence, the NVA firm m_{NVA} induces a characteristic function $v': 2^M \rightarrow \mathbb{R}$ with $v'(J) := v''(J \cup m_{NVA})$ for $J \subseteq M$.

Building on the assumption of limited transparency in hierarchical bargaining structures, I argue that only firms that would be in the same cluster as m_{NVA} if m_{NVA} was not NVA (i.e., their supplies or services are closely connected to the supply of the NVA firm) are aware and take benefit of it. The cluster that would include m_{NVA} is denoted by M_{NVA}. Similarly, starting again from the characteristic function $v'': 2^{M \cup m_{NVA}} \rightarrow \mathbb{R}$ on the set $M \cup m_{NVA}$ in the hypothetical situation that m_{NVA} is not NVA, let $\hat{v}': 2^{\mathfrak{B}} \rightarrow \mathbb{R}$ be the induced characteristic function on L1 defined in the obvious fashion that $\hat{v}'(J) := v''\left(\bigcup_{M_i \in J} M_i \cup m_{NVA}\right)$ if $J \cap \quad {}_{NVA} \neq \emptyset$ and $\hat{v}'(J) := \hat{v}(J)$ if $J \cap M_{NVA} = \emptyset$ for $J \subseteq \mathfrak{B}$. Accordingly, on L2 let $\check{v}''_{M_i}: 2^{M \cup m_{NVA}} \rightarrow \mathbb{R}$ be defined analog to Equation (4) based on the characteristic function v'' if m_{NVA} was not NVA. Consequently, let $\check{v}'_{M_i}: 2^M \rightarrow \mathbb{R}$ be the induced characteristic function defined in the fashion that $\check{v}'_{M_i}(J) := \check{v}''_{M_i}(J \cup m_{NVA})$ if $J \cap M_i \neq \emptyset$ and $\check{v}'_{M_i}(J) := \check{v}''_{M_i}(J)$ if $J \cap M_i = \emptyset$. This means, a firm being part of the cluster M_i will incorporate m_{NVA} into its bargaining position and include it in any coalition of firms $J \subseteq M$.

If m_{NVA} does not belong to any cluster, it would be participating hypothetically in top-level negotiations. Similarly to the non-hierarchical case, I assume that all firms and representatives of clusters participating in L1 negotiations are aware of m_{NVA}, split the free value, and further share it with the firms in their respective cluster.

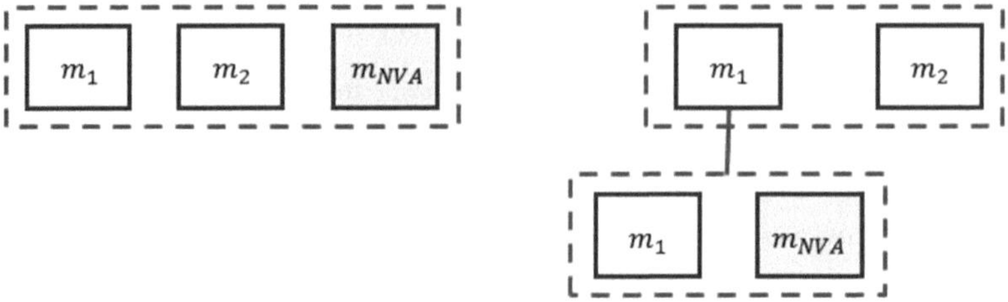

Figure 10: Illustration of the non-hierarchical and hierarchical bargaining structure in the hypothetical case of m_{NVA} being value-appropriating

The following paragraphs analyze which firm in the bargaining structure benefits most from free value provided by an NVA firm. In the most simple case of a (hypothetical) non-hierarchical bargaining structure with two value-appropriating firms m_1, m_2 and one NVA firm m_{NVA} (see Figure 10 for an illustration), both value appropriating firms being aware of the NVA firm and m_1 appropriates $\phi_{m_1}(v') = \frac{1}{2}\big(v''(m_1 m_{NVA}) + v''(m_1 m_2 m_{NVA}) - v''(m_2 m_{NVA})\big)$. In case of m_{NVA} being closely tied to m_1 (hypothetically clustered with m_1 in case of m_{NVA} not being NVA, thus, m_2 not being aware of m_{NVA}), m_1 would capture $\phi_{m_1}^{HSV}(\check{v}'_{M_{NVA}}, \mathfrak{B}) = \phi_{M_{NVA}}(\hat{v}') = \frac{1}{2}\big(v''(m_1 m_{NVA}) + v''(m_1 m_2 m_{NVA}) - v''(m_2)\big)$. Hence, m_1 benefits by directly building on m_{NVA} (and hiding m_{NVA} from m_2) by $\phi_{m_1}^{HSV}(\check{v}'_{M_{NVA}}, \mathfrak{B}) - \phi_{m_1}(v') = v''(m_2 m_{NVA}) - v''(m_2) = \Delta_{m_2, m_{NVA}}$. That is, the benefits of m_1 depend on the complementarity between the other company m_2 and the NVA firm, but not on the complementarity between m_1 and m_{NVA}. The higher the complementarity between m_2 and m_{NVA} the more value is claimed by m_2 in the "non-hierarchical" case, making the other case more attractive for m_1.

Further, starting from the basic bargaining structure with three non-essential, symmetric, and value-appropriating firms $M = \{m_1, m_2, m_3\}$ (in case of hierarchy $\mathfrak{B} = \{\{m_1, m_2\}, m_3\}$), the value chain is extended by an NVA firm m_{NVA} . Let the characteristic function $v'': 2^{M \cup m_{NVA}} \to \mathbb{R}$, for the hypothetical case of m_{NVA} not being NVA, be defined according to Table 12 with $0 < \alpha \leq \beta \leq \gamma \leq 1$.

$J \subseteq M \cup m_{NVA}$	$v''(J)$
$m_{NVA}, m_1, m_2\ m_3$	α
$m_1m_2, m_1m_3, m_1m_{NVA}$, $m_2m_3, m_2m_{NVA}, m_3m_{NVA}$	β
$m_1m_2m_3, m_1m_2m_{NVA}$, $m_1m_3m_{NVA}, m_2m_3m_{NVA}$	γ
$m_1m_2m_3m_{NVA}$	1

Table 12: Characteristic functions $v'': 2^{M \cup m_{NVA}} \to \mathbb{R}$ for a three-firm bargaining structure with NVA firm

In the case of a non-hierarchical bargaining structure, the symmetric non-essential firms share the overall value of the value chain and consequently the additional value provided by m_{NVA}. Each firm appropriates $\phi_{m_1}(v') = \phi_{m_2}(v') = \phi_{m_3}(v') = 1/3$ (with $v'(J) = v''(J \cup m_{NVA})$ defined on M.

In the hierarchical case, there are three different value chain architectures that can be distinguished by the position of m_{NVA} in the hypothetical case of m_{NVA} being value appropriating (see Figure 11).

In the first case, m_{NVA} is not attached to any cluster but added to the overall product in the final integration step. Thus, every participant in top-level negotiation incorporates m_{NVA} into its own position. It holds that firms in the cluster as well as m_3 can appropriate a share of the free value (and thus benefit in absolute terms) if their value add to the remaining system is not significantly lower through the presence of m_{NVA} than in a value chain without m_{NVA}. In detail, m_3 benefits if $1 - \gamma + \beta - \alpha > \gamma - \beta$,

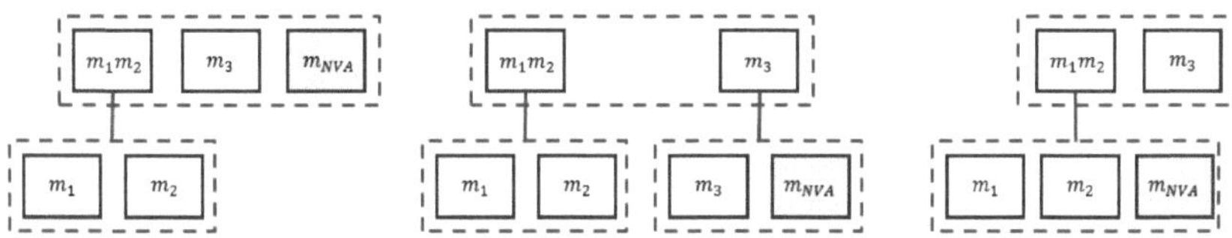

Figure 11: Illustration of the hypothetical hierarchical bargaining structures with the non-value-appropriating firm m_{NVA} being value appropriating

and the firms in the cluster m_1 and m_2 benefit if $1-\beta > \beta - \alpha$. In relative terms, it is likely that the firms in the cluster can benefit disproportionally from m_{NVA}. If $y - \beta > (\beta - \alpha)/\gamma$ holds, which is in particular true for fully complementary value chains, m_1 and m_2 can increase their relative value capture in the value chain.

Second, if m_{NVA} is attached to m_3(creating a hypothetical cluster), it is the only firm to include m_{NVA} in its proposition as other firms are, according to my assumption, not aware of m_{NVA}. Thus, m_3 could increase its value capture share from $1/2 * (\alpha + \gamma - \beta)$ (in the case without NVA) to $1/2$. However, if m_{NVA} sufficiently increases the value to be distributed, m_1 and m_2 may benefit as well from m_{NVA} in absolute terms (although having a smaller share of the overall value). This is the case if $1 - \beta > \gamma - \alpha$, that is, if the value add of the m_1-m_2-cluster to the m_3-m_{NVA}-cluster is higher than that to the stand-alone firm m_3.

Third, if m_1 and m_2 form a joint cluster with m_{NVA}, they both disproportionally benefit from the free value and increase their share of value capture. Similar to the last case, m_3 benefits if the presence of m_{NVA} in the value chain increases its value add to the remaining system, that is if $1 - \gamma > \gamma - \beta$.

The results indicate that it is beneficial to be directly clustered with the NVA firm. The example of two value-appropriating firms shows that the higher the complementarity between m_{NVA} and other firms or clusters that are not aware of m_{NVA}, the more beneficial it is to incorporate (and integrate) the NVA firm's proposition. Moreover, other firms may benefit as well from the presence of the NVA firm if it increases their marginal contribution to the value chain.

PROPOSITION 9: *In a bargaining structure with two or three value-appropriating firms and an NVA firm, firms benefit from the presence of the NVA firm in the value chain by directly building on and including it in their proposition. The example with two value-appropriating firms shows that the higher the complementarity, in particular between the NVA firm and the other firm, the more beneficial it is for the focal firm to create a (hypothetical) cluster with the NVA firm. Nevertheless, other firms may benefit from the presence of the NVA firm in the value chain if it increases their value add to the system.*

The results complement existing literature on how commercial firms can benefit from open source developments. Providing complementary products and services in addition to an open source product or enhancing the own product through open source complements are ways to monetize open source developments (Lerner and Tirole 2002; Raymond 1999). In addition, the results show that firms automatically share the benefits from the open source development with other companies in the value chain. A firm benefits most if is the only one to directly build on the open source product and conceals the presence of the non-value-appropriating firm to other participants in the bargaining structure.

4.4 Alternative distribution concepts

In the following section alternative hierarchical value distribution concepts are discussed. The first part focuses on the most important modifications of the Shapley value for hierarchical bargaining structures, in collaborative game theory so-called a priori coalition structures. In particular, applicability and results of the Owen value (Owen 1977) and the $\mathfrak{B}$-value (Aumann and Drèze 1974) are analyzed.

Further, another prominent concept in cooperative game theory, namely the Core, is discussed. I evaluate its applicability for hierarchical bargaining structures, analyze Pulido and Sánchez-Sorino's (2009) hierarchal extension, and derive the Hierarchical Core concept that fits the specific requirements.

Although knowing that there is an even broader range of cooperative game theoretic concepts, such as the Kernel, the Bargaining Set, the Nucleolus, or the Banzhaf value, I restrict myself to two most important ones—the Shapley value and the Core.

4.4.1 Owen value

The concept of the Owen value (OV) (Owen 1977) is similar to the HSV, however it differs in an important respect. It can also be seen as a two-step approach. First, the overall value is split on top-level according to the Shapley value. Second, the value allocated to any cluster is further split among all firms contained in the focal cluster by a variation of the Shapley value.

The value distribution on level-1 is analogue to the L1-HSV (see Section 4.1.2, Equation (3)). That is, a cluster $M_i \in \mathfrak{B}$ captures

$$\phi_{M_i}(\hat{v}) := \sum_{S \subseteq \mathfrak{B} \setminus \{M_i\}} \frac{|S|!\,(k - |S| - 1)!}{k!} \big(\hat{v}(S \cup M_i) - \hat{v}(S)\big).$$

In the second step, again the Shapley value concept is used to determine the distribution of value allocated to a cluster M_i among the firms that are part of M_i. In contrast to the HSV, in which a firm assumes that all other clusters participate in the value chain, the OV is defined via the value add to all possibly incomplete value chains. That is, the value capture of a firm according to Owen takes the distribution game among clusters into account.

Compared to the HSV, the OV fits a setting with a higher level of transparency. While the HSV reflects a bargaining structure in which firms not involved in top-level bargaining have no transparency of these negotiations and assume the complete bargaining structure in place, the OV reflects a setting in which firms in a cluster have some information on the negotiations conducted on top-level. In detail, a firm that is part of a cluster knows the value add of every other clusters (to any possibly incomplete set of clusters) in the top-level negotiation and assess its "fair" share based on this information. That is, the firm considers its value add to the potentially incomplete value chain. Note that in both concepts a firm being part of a cluster has full transparency on the negotiations and players (including value add) within its cluster.

Formally, the OV uses an adapted Shapely value distribution for the L1 game evaluating all combinations of clusters (excluding the focal cluster M_i). That is for every $S \subseteq M_i$ the characteristic function $v_S^{M_i}: 2^{\mathfrak{B}} \to \mathbb{R}$ is defined. Let $\bar{S}$ be the complement of S in M_i, so $\bar{S} = M_i \backslash S$. For $J \subseteq \mathfrak{B}$:

$$v_S^{M_i}(J) := v\left(\bigcup_{M_l \in J} M_l \backslash \bar{S}\right)$$

This means, if $M_i \in J$ the characteristic function for the set of all cluster in J without M_i but including S is evaluated.

Further, the characteristic function $v^{M_i}: 2^{M_i} \to \mathbb{R}$ is used for the game within M_i. For $S \subseteq M_i$ let be:

$$v^{M_i}(S) := \phi_{M_i}(v_S^{M_i})$$

The (L2-) OV for a firm $m_j \in M_i$ is defined as:

$$\phi_{m_j}^{OV}(v) := \phi_{m_j}^{OV}(v^{M_i}) = \sum_{S \subseteq M_i \backslash \{m_j\}} \frac{|S|!\,(|M_i| - |S| - 1)!}{|M_i|!} \left(v^{M_i}(S \cup \{m_j\}) - v^{M_i}(S)\right) \tag{17}$$

Note that the OV satisfies efficiency related to the overall value chain, that is, $\sum_{m_j \in M} \phi_{m_j}^{OV}(v) = v(N)$, and within each cluster, that is, $\sum_{m_j \in M_i} \phi_{m_j}^{OV}(v) = \phi_{M_i}(\hat{v})$. Further, similar to the Shapley value it satisfies additivity, invariance under dummy players and an adapted version of symmetry, called symmetry across coalitions and symmetry within coalitions. Aumann and Drèze (1974) as well as Hart and Kurz (1983) show that these attributes uniquely define the OV.

In the end, how real-world hierarchical bargaining settings can be best modeled is an empirical question. It is open to check empirically whether results of real negotiations can be explained by one of the value distribution concepts. Nevertheless, I see the HSV as the appropriate concept to reflect negotiation situations with limited information for individual players. The assumption of not knowing (or ignoring) the negotiations on top-level is plausible especially when thinking of step-wise value distribution. After top-level negotiations, firms within every cluster can see the presence of the complete rest of the value chain (all other clusters) as given.

The remainder of this section aims at getting a better understanding of the differences between HSV and OV by analyzing some bargaining structures from Section 4.2 with the OV.

First, in the simple three-firm bargaining structure introduced in Section 4.2.1 one can see a difference in the pattern of who benefits from hierarchy. Based on the introduced characteristic function (see Table 1) and the respective OV value distribution (see Table 13), the results (see Table 14) show that there is a difference in the case of exactly one essential firm not being part of a cluster.

In contrast to the HSV results in Section 4.2.1, both firms in the large cluster $m_1 m_2$ benefit from hierarchy if $1 - \beta < \beta - \alpha$ (Function 3), that is, if the value add of a second firm ($\beta - \alpha$) is smaller than the value add of third firm (see Figure 12).

Further, an important take-away from analyzing larger bargaining structures (see Section 4.2.2 and Appendix E) with the OV is the limited difference between HSV and OV results. As value capture differs between the HSV and OV, the answer to the question whether for a firm the given hierarchical bargaining structure is more favorable than a non-hierarchical one differs as well. For example, while in cases in which the essential firm E is clustered with many non-essential firms (Case E in the evaluation, see Table 6 and Table 24) at a low level of complementarity ($x = 1.5$) the hierarchical bargaining structure is favorable for E according to HSV, the non-hierarchical structure

# ess. firms		L1-OV of...		L2-HSV of firms in m_1m_2	
m_1m_2	m_3	m_1m_2	m_3	Essential	Non-essential
0	0	$\frac{1}{2}(1-\alpha+\beta)$	$\frac{1}{2}(1+\alpha-\beta)$	-	$\frac{1}{4}(1-\alpha+\beta)$
1	0	$\frac{1}{2}(1+\beta)$	$\frac{1}{2}(1-\beta)$	$\frac{1}{4}(1+\alpha+2\beta)$	$\frac{1}{4}(1-\alpha)$
0	1	$\frac{1}{2}(1-\alpha)$	$\frac{1}{2}(1+\alpha)$	-	$\frac{1}{4}(1-\alpha)$
2	0	$\frac{1}{2}(1+\beta)$	$\frac{1}{2}(1-\beta)$	$\frac{1}{4}(1+\beta)$	-
1	1	$\frac{1}{2}$	$\frac{1}{2}$	$\frac{1}{4}(1+\beta)$	$\frac{1}{4}(1-\beta)$
2	1	$\frac{1}{2}$	$\frac{1}{2}$	$\frac{1}{4}$	-

Table 13: OV for clusters and firms in a three-firm bargaining structure

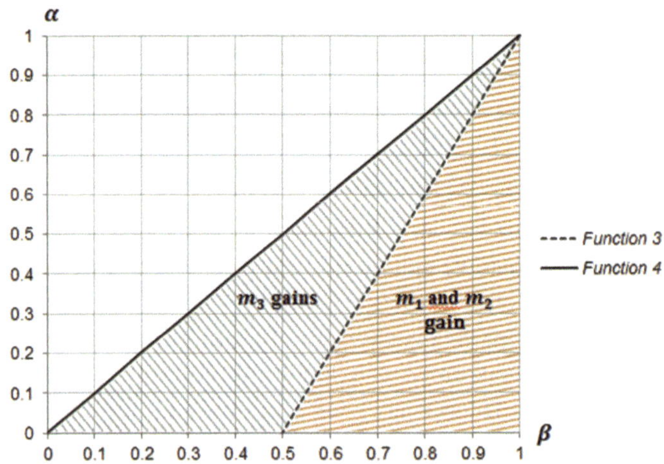

Figure 12: Analysis of three-firm bargaining structures with one essential firm with OV: Which firms benefit from hierarchy?

# essential firms in $m_1 m_2$	m_3	**Who gains and who loses through hierarchy (OV scenario)**
1	0	The **essential firm in $m_1 m_2$** gains if and only if $\frac{1}{4}(1+\alpha+2\beta) > \frac{1}{3}(1+\alpha+\beta) \Leftrightarrow 1-\beta < \beta-\alpha \Leftrightarrow \alpha < 2\beta-1$, this is if and only if the value add is larger in the first step (for every two firms) than in the second step (from two to three firms). The **non-essential firm in $m_1 m_2$** gains if and only if $\frac{1}{4}(1-\alpha) > \frac{1}{6}(2-\alpha-\beta) \Leftrightarrow 1-\beta < \beta-\alpha \Leftrightarrow \alpha < 2\beta-1$, this is if and only if the value add is larger in the first step (for every two firms) than in the second step (from two to three firms)—and whenever the essential firm in $m_1 m_2$ gains. The **non-essential firm outside $m_1 m_2$** gains if and only if $\frac{1}{2}(1-\beta) > \frac{1}{6}(2-\alpha-\beta) \Leftrightarrow 1-\beta > \beta-\alpha \Leftrightarrow \alpha > 2\beta-1$, this is if and only if the value add is larger in the second step (from two to three firms) than in the first step (for every two firms)
Other		Analog to HSV (Table 4)

Table 14: Analysis of three-firm bargaining structure with OV: Which firms benefit from hierarchy?

is beneficial in cases of full transparency, that is, according to OV. However, the most beneficial bargaining structure for a certain firm is identical in both concepts: for the essential firm *E* the bargaining structure with a stand-alone position in top-level negotiations and all other firms being part of a single cluster is most beneficial; for a non-essential firm *N* the hierarchical bargaining structure in which *N* is directly participates in top-level negotiations while all other firms are clustered with the essential firm is the most beneficial setup. Moreover, the difference between HSV and OV is at the maximum 2.8% of the overall value captured by the value chain. Further, with increasing size of the value chain or increasing levels of complementarity the value captures for HSV and OV converge.

4.4.2 $\mathfrak{B}$-value

The $\mathfrak{B}$-value, introduced by Aumann and Drèze (1974) focuses solely on value distribution within each cluster of firms, disregarding the distribution on top-level. For a firm m_j being part of the cluster $M_i \in \mathfrak{B}$ let $\phi_{m_j}^{M_i}$ denote the value capture of $m_j \subseteq M_i$ in the distribution game within the cluster M_i according to Shapley. In addition, the restricted characteristic function $v|_{M_i}: 2^{M_i} \rightarrow \mathbb{R}$ is defined by $v|_{M_i}(S) = v(S)$ for all $S \subseteq M_i$. The $\mathfrak{B}$-value for $m_j \in M_i$ is defined as:

$$\phi_{m_j}^{\mathfrak{B}}(v) := \phi_{m_j}^{M_i}(v|_{M_i}) = \sum_{S \subseteq M_i \backslash \{m_j\}} \frac{|S|!\,(|M_i| - |S| - 1)!}{|M_i|!} (v|_{M_i}(S \cup \{m_j\}) - v|_{M_i}(S)) \tag{18}$$

The most interesting attribute of the $\mathfrak{B}$-value is that in contrast to the HSV and Shapley value it only satisfies relative efficiency, which is $\sum_{m_j \in M_i} \phi_{m_j}^{M_i}(v|_{M_i}) = v(M_j)$, but not efficiency. This implies that value is not distributed across the total bargaining structure as transfers of value to other clusters are not intended (Winter 2002). Value not allocated to any cluster, $v(M) - \sum_{M_j \in \mathfrak{B}} v(M_j)$, could be interpreted as the value appropriated by the architect or integrator of the overall value chain (as the surplus that is created by the architecture).

However, an important drawback of the $\mathfrak{B}$-value by Aumann and Drèze is the limited applicability for cases of complementary or substitutionary effects, in particular if these are not constrained to a single cluster. The $\mathfrak{B}$-value does not take the effect of firms outside the focal cluster into account. As a consequence, in a bargaining structure with essential firms (that is, there exists $C_e \subseteq M$ such that $v(J) = 0 \; if \; C_e \nsubseteq J$) that are not all contained in a single cluster, the characteristic function will always provide trivial results (i.e., zero) if only firms within the focal cluster are considered for value distribution.[34] Similarly, in the case of substitute firms a cluster might in sum claim more

---

[34] Assuming that the bargaining structure M consists of $p \geq 2$ essential firms $C_e = \{m_j\}_{j \in \{1,\ldots,p\}}$ which are part of different level-1 cluster, for example, let $m_1 \in M_1$ and $m_2 \in M_2$. Calculating the characteristic function for any subset $S \subseteq M_1$ would result in a value of 0 as the other essential firms m_2 is not part of the focal subset.

value than it appropriates in the overall system as the $\mathfrak{B}$-value disregards substitution effects across clusters.[35] This makes the $\mathfrak{B}$-value useless to estimate value distributions in real value chains and bargaining structures.

4.4.3 Hierarchical Core

Besides the Shapley value, the Core (Shapley 1952; Gillies 1953) is one of the most well-known solution concepts in cooperative game theory. The Core circumscribes a set of stable value allocations which no subset of players can improve upon, that is every group of firms achieves the highest value capture possible given the strategy of other firms in the bargaining structure. In contrast to the Shapley value, the Core does not provide a single value distribution but a set of possible outcomes of negotiations that is possibly empty. In general, the Shapley value is not a Core allocation rule. However, for complementary value chains the Core is non-empty and the Shapley value distribution will be among the Core solutions (as complementarity among all subset of firms is represented in a convex characteristic function) (Shapley 1971). Further, some studies indicate a lower predictive accuracy of the Core compared to the Shapley value (Murnighan and Roth 1977; Michener et al. 1983),[36] which is a key reason for choosing the Shapley concept as the basis for my analyses (in addition to the difficulties resulting from a set of possible outcomes in contrast to a single value).

Formally, the Core is defined for a game with a set of firms M and a characteristic function $v: 2^M \rightarrow \mathbb{R}$. Let $x \in \mathbb{R}^{|M|}$ be the vector of value capture of all firms in M and $x(J) := \sum_{i \in J} x_i$ the total value capture of a group of firms $J \subseteq M$. The Core is defined as

$$C(M, v) = \{x \in \mathbb{R}^{|M|} | x(J) \geq v(J)\ \forall J \subset M \ and\ x(M) = v(M)\}. \tag{19}$$

---

[35] Let $C_s = \{m_j\}_{j \in \{1,\dots,p\}} \subseteq M$ be substitute firms, i.e. $m_1, m_2 \in C_s$ then $v(J \cup \{m_2\}) = v(J), \forall J \subseteq M : m_1 \in J$. If m_1, m_2 are in the same cluster, they split the value they add to the value chain. However, if they are in different cluster both claim the full value. Hence, $v(M_1) + v(M_2) \geq v(M_1 \cup M_2)$, with $m_1 \in M_1, m_2 \in M_2$.

[36] Predictive accuracy is indicated by the mean goodness-of-fit score. For imputation theories, that is, theories that suggest a point solution, goodness-of-fit scores measure the Euclidian distance between the observed and predicted results. The goodness-of-fit score used for the Core takes, in addition, the size of the predicted solution space into account. For details, I refer to Bonacich (1979).

As said above, the Core provides a set of plausible and stable value distributions. A Core distribution is not necessarily fair (as the SV claims to be) and therefore may not fulfill the properties of symmetry, additivity, and invariance under dummy players (see Section 4.1.1).

To analyze hierarchical bargaining structures with the Core concept, I now turn to hierarchical extensions. In literature, Pulido and Sánchez-Soriano (2009) as well as Aumann and Drèze (1974) provide modifications of the Core concept for a priori coalition structures. Analog to Owen and the HSV, they model the game as a two-step procedure with a Core allocation of value both on top-level and within each cluster.

In detail, the Coalitional Core suggested by Pulido and Sánchez-Soriano (2009) for a set of firms M, a bargaining structure $\mathfrak{B} = \{M_1, \dots, M_k\}$, and a characteristic function $v: 2^M \to \mathbb{R}$ uses again the induced characteristic function $\hat{v}: 2^{\mathfrak{B}} \to \mathbb{R}, \hat{v}(J) := v\left(\bigcup_{M_i \in J} M_i\right)$ for value distribution on top-level (analog to the HSV and OV—see Section 4.1.2 and 4.4.1). I assume that there is an allocation of the value on top-level according to the Core, that is, there is $y \in \mathbb{R}^{\mathrm{k}}$ with $y \in C(\mathfrak{B}, \hat{v})$.

In the second step the value is distributed among the firms participating in the focal cluster. Pulido and Sánchez-Soriano introduce the induced characteristic function $v_{M_i}^y: 2^{M_i} \to \mathbb{R}$ on M_i with

$$v_{M_i}^y(J) := \begin{cases} y_i & if\ J = M_i \\ \max\limits_{S \subseteq \mathfrak{B} \setminus M_i} \left\{ v\left(\bigcup\limits_{M_j \in S} M_j \cup J \right) - y(S) \right\} & if\ J \subsetneq M_i. \end{cases}$$

Assuming that the allocation of value within every cluster follows the Core concept, the Coalitional Core is defined as

$$CC(M, v, \mathfrak{B}) = \bigcup_{y \in C(\mathfrak{B}, \hat{v})} \bigotimes_{i=1:k} C\left(M_i, v_{M_i}^y\right), \tag{20}$$

which is equivalent to

$$\left\{ x \in \mathbb{R}^{|M|} \middle| x(M) = v(M), x(J) \geq v(J) \forall J \in \Omega_{\mathfrak{B}} \right\} \tag{21}$$

with $\Omega_{\mathfrak{B}} = \left\{ J \subseteq M \middle| J = P \cup Q\ with\ P \subseteq M_i, Q = \bigcup_{M_j \in S} M_j\ \ with\ S \subseteq \mathfrak{B} \setminus M_i, M_i \in \mathfrak{B} \right\}$.

However, the Coalitional Core does not reflect my basic assumptions with regard to the level of transparency for firms throughout the value chain (see Section 4.1.2, pg. 22).

Similar to the Own value, it reflects negotiations in which firms that are part of a particular cluster have full information on top-level negotiations and do not take the presence of all other clusters as given.[37]

Therefore, I define the Hierarchical Core (HC), which is an extension of the Core concept similar to the Coalitional Core, reflecting the basic assumption of limited information for firms that are part of a cluster (and are only involved in L2 negotiations). While the set of possible outcomes in top-level negotiations is analog to the Coalitional Core, the induced characteristic function $v_{M_i}^{y\,*}: 2^{M_i} \rightarrow \mathbb{R}$ is defined for negotiations within M_i as

$$v_{M_i}^{y\,*}(J) := \begin{cases} y_i & if\, J = M_i \\ \max\{0; v(J \cup M \backslash M_i) - y(M \backslash M_i)\} & if\, J \subset M_i. \end{cases}$$

Consequently, the HC is defined as

$$HC(M, v, \mathfrak{B}) = \bigcup_{y \in C(\mathfrak{B}, \hat{v})} \bigotimes_{i=1:k} C(M_i, v_{M_i}^{y\,*}) \tag{22}$$

which is equivalent to

$$\{x \in \mathbb{R}^{|M|} | x(M) = v(M), x(J) \geq v(J) \forall J \in \Omega_{\mathfrak{B}}^*\} \tag{23}$$

with $\Omega_{\mathfrak{B}}^* = \{R \subseteq M | R = K \cup M/M_i \; with \; K \subseteq M_i, M_i \in \mathfrak{B}\}$ (see Appendix F for a proof of the equivalence).

In the following the basic three-firm bargaining structure from Section 4.2.1 is analyzed to get a better understanding of the HC and its link to the HSV. The analysis will show that changes in value capture due to a change in the hierarchical bargaining structure predicted by the HSV are not necessarily reflected in the respective Core/HC solution spaces.

I focus on the example with three symmetric non-essential firms N_1, N_2, N_3, a hierarchical bargaining structure $\mathfrak{B} = \{N_1, \{N_2, N_3\}\}$, a characteristic function defined

---

[37] Similarly, the Core for a priori coalition structures defined by Aumann and Drèze (1974) assumes increased transparency for firms participating in a cluster. Moreover, firms consider not only the top-level negotiations but also possibilities beyond the a priori structure. Therefore, I will not delve into this concept.

	Shapley and Core distributions
Non-hierarchical bargaining structure	$\phi_{N_1}(v) = \phi_{N_2}(v) = \phi_{N_3}(v) = \frac{1}{3}$
	$C(M,v) = \{x \in \mathbb{R}^3 \mid x_{N_1} + x_{N_2} + x_{N_3} = 1, x_{N_1} \geq \alpha, x_{N_2} \geq \alpha, x_{N_3} \geq \alpha,$ $x_{N_1} + x_{N_2} \geq \beta, x_{N_1} + x_{N_3} \geq \beta, x_{N_2} + x_{N_3} \geq \beta\}$
Hierarchical bargaining structure	$\phi_{N_1}(\hat{v}, \mathfrak{B}) = \frac{1}{2}(1 + \alpha - \beta), \quad \phi_{N_2N_3}(\hat{v}, \mathfrak{B}) = \frac{1}{2}(1 - \alpha + \beta)$ $\phi_{N_2}^{HSV}(v) = \phi_{N_3}^{HSV}(v) = \frac{1}{4}(1 - \alpha + \beta)$
	$C(\mathfrak{B}, \hat{v}) = \{(y_{N_1}, y_{N_2N_3}) \in \mathbb{R}^2 \mid y(M) = 1, y_{N_1} \geq \alpha, y_{N_2N_3} \geq \beta\}$ $HC(M, v, \mathfrak{B}) = \bigcup_{y \in C(\mathfrak{B},\hat{v})} \{x_{N_1} \in \mathbb{R} \mid x_{N_1} = y_{N_1}\} \otimes \{(x_{N_2}, x_{N_3})$ $\in \mathbb{R}^2 \mid x_{N_2} + x_{N_3} = y_{N_2N_3}, x_{N_2} \geq \max\{0; \beta - y_{N_1}\}, x_{N_3}$ $\geq \max\{0; \beta - y_{N_1}\}\}$

Table 15: Non-hierarchical and hierarchical Shapley and Core value distributions for a three-firm bargaining structure with non-essential symmetric firms

according to Table 1, and the hierarchical and non-hierarchical Shapley and Core distributions (see Table 15).

In the following, I show that the HSV is part of the HC if the value chain is complementary (i.e., $1 - \beta \geq \beta - \alpha \geq \alpha$, which results in a convex characteristic function). First, it is obvious that on top-level $(\phi_{N_1}^{HSV}, \phi_{N_2N_3}^{HSV}) \in C(\mathfrak{B}, \hat{v})$ in case of strict complementarity. Second, in order to demonstrate that $(\phi_{N_1}^{HSV}, \phi_{N_2}^{HSV}, \phi_{N_3}^{HSV}) \in HC(M, v, \mathfrak{B})$, I need to show that $(\phi_{N_2}^{HSV}, \phi_{N_3}^{HSV}) \in \{(x_{N_2}, x_{N_3}) \in \mathbb{R}^2 \mid x_{N_2} + x_{N_3} = y_{N_2N_3}, x_{N_2} \geq \max\{0; \beta - y_{N_1}\}, x_{N_3} \geq \max\{0; \beta - y_{N_1}\}\}$, that is $\phi_{N_2}^{HSV} \geq \beta - \phi_{N_1}^{HSV}$ and $\phi_{N_3}^{HSV} \geq \beta - \phi_{N_1}^{HSV}$ (as $\phi_{N_2}^{HSV}, \phi_{N_3}^{HSV} \geq 0$).

As $\frac{1}{4}(1 - \alpha + \beta) \geq \beta - \frac{1}{2}(1 + \alpha - \beta) \Leftrightarrow 3(1 - \beta) \geq 2\beta - \alpha$ and $1 - \beta \geq \beta - \alpha$ it is sufficient to show that $2(\beta - \alpha) \geq \beta$ holds. As $\beta = \alpha + (\beta - \alpha)$ and $\beta - \alpha \geq \alpha$ holds because of complementarity, it is shown that in this case the HSV allocation is part of the HC value distributions. However, note that in general strict complementarity does not necessarily imply that the HSV is part of the HC.

Further, for a given $y \in C(\mathfrak{B}, \hat{v})$ the HC will be empty if $y_{N_1} + 2(\beta - y_{N_1}) > 1$, that is, if $2\beta - 1 > y_{N_1}$. As $y_{N_1} \geq \alpha$, it follows that the HC is empty if $\beta - \alpha \geq 1 - \beta$, that is, if there is no complementarity in the step from two to three firms. One could interpret an empty HC as an unstable bargaining structure (and value chain) with some firms not being satisfied with their current value capture.

In the following, I aim to understand if the effect of bargaining structures on value appropriation that was identified using the Shapley value concept, is also reflected in the Core concept. Therefore, the Core, HC, SV and HSV are evaluated for different combinations of α and β to see whether a change in a firm's value capture due to a more (or less) hierarchical bargaining structure implies as well a change of the boundaries of the firm's Core/HC solution space.

As learnt in Section 4.2.1, N_1 benefits from the hierarchical bargaining structure if $\beta - \alpha < \frac{1}{3}$, while N_2 and N_3 lose at the same time. Even if $\phi_{N_1} < \phi_{N_1}^{HSV}$ holds, $\alpha \leq x_{N_1} \leq 1 - \beta$ are the binding restrictions with regard to x_{N_1} both in the non-hierarchical and hierarchical Core. Thus, the change in bargaining structure does not affect the range of possible value capture of N_1.

To understand implications of the change in bargaining structure on the Core solution spaces of the other firms forming a cluster, the possible value capture of N_2 and N_3 in the non-hierarchical and hierarchical bargaining structure is graphically displayed. Based on all important boundary conditions referring to N_2 and N_3 (Table 16) the Core and HC solution space restricted to the x_{N_2}-x_{N_3}-hyperplane with different values of $\beta - \alpha$ is plotted in Figure 13. While N_1 can benefit from hierarchy in Case A since $\beta - \alpha < \frac{1}{3}$ holds, N_2 and N_3 benefit from hierarchy in Case B and C. Although in Cases B and C $\beta - \alpha$ is the same (at 5/12 of the total value), Case C represents a value chain with a lower level of complementarity. In Case C complementarity is only 50% ($= 1 - 3\alpha$) of the overall value while in Case B it is 75%.

One can observe that in Case A and B the Core solution space differs from the HC solution space. In Case A the solution space expands downwards (in the direction of lower value capture) with increasing hierarchy, which is in line with the shift of the expected value capture of the firms according to Shapley (as $\beta - \alpha < \frac{1}{3}$). However, in Case B a similar expansion of the solution space can be observed although there is an upward shift of the Shapley value with the change from a non-hierarchical to a

	Core	HC[38]
(1)	$x_{N_2} + x_{N_3} \geq \beta$	$x_{N_2} + x_{N_3} \geq \beta$
(2)	$x_{N_1} + x_{N_2} + x_{N_3} = 1, x_{N_1} \geq \alpha$ $=> x_{N_2} + x_{N_3} \leq 1 - \alpha$	$x_{N_2} + x_{N_3} \leq 1 - \alpha$
(3)	$x_{N_1} + x_{N_2} + x_{N_3} = 1, x_{N_1} + x_{N_3} \geq \beta$ $=> x_{N_2} \leq 1 - \beta$	$x_{N_2} \leq 1 - \beta$
(4)	$x_{N_3} \leq 1 - \beta$	$x_{N_3} \leq 1 - \beta$
(5)	$x_{N_2} \geq \alpha$	
(6)	$x_{N_3} \geq \alpha$	

Table 16: Important boundary conditions of Core and HC solution space referring to N_2 and N_3

hierarchical bargaining structure can be observed. In addition, in Case C the solution space of Core and HC are identical although the Shapley value concept indicates a shift.

Hence, I can conclude that a change of the expected value capture based on the HSV due to hierarchy is not necessarily reflected in the space of possible value distributions according to the HC. Even if the Core and HC solution spaces change, the change may not be in line with the expected shift in value capture according to Shapley.

Nevertheless, this result does not weaken the suggested impact of hierarchy in bargaining structures on value capture. First, the value distributions suggested by the Core and HC are not necessarily uniformly distributed, that is, not all value distributions in the Core or HC are equally likely. Michener et al. (1979) find in their experiment that the size of the Core has no effect on the probability of a Core distribution being selected. Thus, a difference in the sizes of the Core and HC does not necessarily imply a shift in

38 Note that the inequalities $x_{N_2} \geq \max\{0, \beta - y_{N_1}\}$ and $x_{N_3} \geq \max\{0, \beta - y_{N_1}\}$ are satisfied and hence unnecessary as $x_{N_2} \leq 1 - \beta$, $x_{N_3} \leq 1 - \beta$, and $x_{N_2} + x_{N_3} = 1 - y_{N_1}$ holds

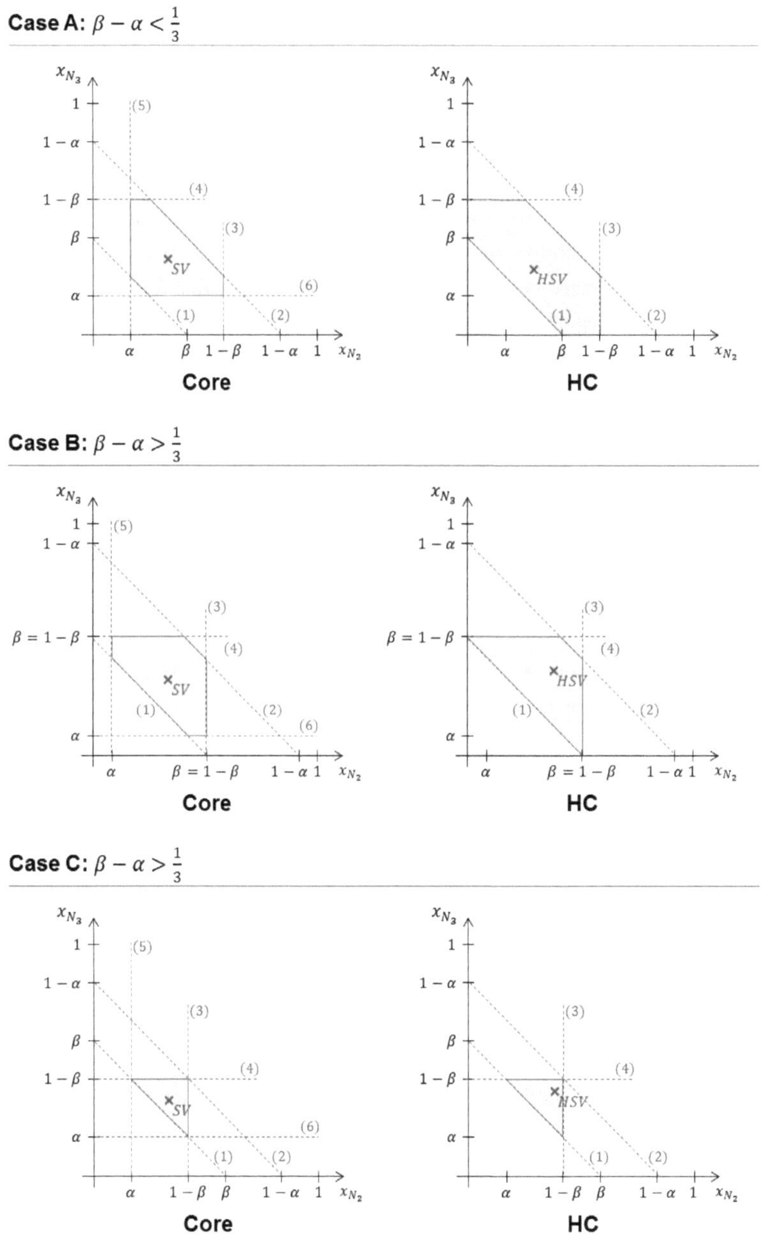

Figure 13: Possible value capture of N_2 and N_3 in the non-hierarchical and hierarchical bargaining structure according to Core and HC concepts

the expected value distribution.[39] Second, as stated above, studies indicate that the Core has lower predictive accuracy than other solution concepts, such as the SV or Nucleolus (Murnighan and Roth 1977; Michener et al. 1983). The theoretical concept assumes that players act individually, collectively and coalitionally rationally—an idea that players do not always follow in reality.

Nevertheless, the Core concept (including the HC) is useful in the present context because it indicates the stability of the bargaining structure. As it provides value distributions that can be accepted by all participating firms, it may reveal potential deviators that have better options apart from the current setup. Thus, it could be used to foresee and manage possible changes of the value chain and bargaining structure.

4.5 Conclusion

The results in the previous sections show that bargaining structure has an effect on value capture. Based on the HSV, the results indicate that a bargaining structure is beneficial for a firm if it participates in the negotiations in which most complementarity is realized. Consequently, in cases of essential firms being part of the bargaining structure non-essential firms benefit if they are directly involved in top-level negotiations. The same holds for essential firms if there is more than one essential firm in the bargaining structure. In return, if most complementarity is realized on the lower level of the bargaining structure, within a particular cluster, being part of the negotiations within this cluster is beneficial with regard to value capture.

In bargaining structures with a single essential firm and exponentially increasing complementarity towards the top-level the focal firm can enhance value capture through consolidating clusters. This setting mirrors a bargaining structure and value chain with a strong, non-replaceable OEM. The OEM can increase value capture through consolidating direct non-essential (keeping all other things, in particular replaceability, constant).

Further, if a firm owns multiple positions in the bargaining structure the decision whether to consolidate has an impact on value capture. Keeping two positions on

---

[39] In contrast, the Core-Center defined by González-Díaz and Sánchez-Rodrígues (2007) takes on the idea of a uniform probability distribution on the Core set and hence suggests the center of gravity as most likely outcome.

different levels separate (potentially through selling for a fair price, that is, a price that reflects the value capture) can be beneficial, in particular, if most complementarity is realized on top-level of the (unconsolidated) bargaining structure.

Not all firms in the value chain are necessarily included in the bargaining structure. Firms that are easily replaceable, for example, due to strong competition, or suppliers of open-source inputs do not appropriate any value although they contribute to value creation. Firms in the bargaining structure can appropriate a share of this free value. As presumably only firms that are close to the focal input generating free value are aware of the non-value-appropriating character of the firm, firms should directly build on these component to maximize value capture. Nevertheless, firms in the rest of the bargaining structure might benefit as well, in particular if their value add increases through the presence of the non-value-appropriating firm.

Based on the relatively strong predictive accuracy of the SV, it is plausible that the HSV is an indicator similar quality for value distribution in hierarchical bargaining structures. Likewise, the Owen value that is also based on the SV but assumes higher transparency for firms, predicts that changes in the bargaining structure affect value capture.

For the well-known Core concept and its extension to hierarchical bargaining structures a change in bargaining structures might affect the boundaries of the solution space, but systematic shifts that are in line with the changes in value capture predicted by the HSV, could not be observed. However, as the possible value distributions provided by the Core are not necessarily uniformly distributed, the boundaries of the Core solution space have little explanatory value.

5 Drivers of bargaining structure and empirical implications of the hierarchy strategy

While the last chapter showed that bargaining structure should matter for value capture, the present chapter examines the drivers of bargaining structures with an aim to understand if and how firms use them. As the position of a firm in the bargaining structure and the degree of hierarchy affects the share of value captured, firms should seek to influence the bargaining structure to their own advantage. However, it remains to be discussed whether firms actively shape the bargaining structure, which levers they apply, and if their action is in line with the hierarchy strategy. In an attempt to answer these questions I use a qualitative research approach with case studies examining the value chains and bargaining structures of laundry dryers produced by Bosch Siemens Hausgeräte GmbH (BSH) and of large passenger aircrafts, in particular the Airbus A350 and the Boeing 787 Dreamliner.

All in all, based on the discussion and development of tentative answers in Section 3.2, the following research questions are in focus:

- What are the drivers of bargaining structure?
- To what extent does the bargaining structure mirror the value chain architecture?
- Do firms actively manage the bargaining structure? What levers do they apply?
- If firms actively manage the bargaining structure, are their actions in line with the hierarchy strategy?

Note that determining the effects of changes in the bargaining structure on value capture is beyond the scope of this study. The impact of bargaining structures on value capture can hardly be analyzed in real-world settings as it is difficult to assess the value capture of a specific firm and almost impossible to do so for all firms within a given value chain. The assessment of value capture requires much confidential information, such as the overall real cost base or purchasing and sales contracts. Even if a single firm provided researchers full transparency, one could not assess the share of value captured from the total value created along the value chain. In addition, changes in the bargaining structure typically go hand-in-hand with other changes in such areas as product design or the division of labor. These changes, in turn, affect value distribution; for example, the acquisition of new capabilities by a firm can have an impact on the replaceability of multiple firms in the value chain, or a change in product quality can affect the complementarity generated. Further, estimating value capture through public information is nearly impossible as the value a firm appropriates is not only represented in profits but is also partly further distributed to stakeholders such as employees or shareholders. Hence, I deal solely with pointing out actual changes in bargaining structures and illustrating the effects based on the game theoretic model developed in the last chapter.

5.1 Methods

To my knowledge, the investigated topic—the interplay between value chain/ product architecture and bargaining structure, as well as the hierarchy strategy—has not yet been the focus of research. Based on existing literature and logical arguing, I was able to derive first hypotheses on the drivers of bargaining structures (see Section 3.2) and their effects on value capture. Hence, following Edmondson and McMannus (2007), I chose a qualitative research approach to further explore the phenomenon and develop new answers or refine the tentative ones. According to Corbin and Strauss (2008) and Yin (1984), a case study is the appropriate method used to uncover the motivation of participants, to understand why decisions are made, and to illustrate the effects of these decisions. Therefore, in my view, a case study is the most appropriate method to use to capture a thorough understanding of the determinants of bargaining structures, the interactions of participating firms, the reasons for their actions, and their effects.

It is important to discuss how to ensure the quality of qualitative research method. Methodological rigor in management case studies focusing on nascent and intermediate research fields is critical, as the generated hypotheses build the starting point for further research (Eisenhardt and Graebner 2007). Conversely, deficiencies can weaken the recommendations derived for practitioners. I follow the criteria suggested by Campbell (1975), Campbell and Stanley (1963), and described in Gibbert et al. (2008) to assess the rigor: internal validity, external validity, and reliability.[40]

First, internal validity refers to a compelling logical argumentation of the researcher that explains the empirical research conclusions. On the one hand, internal validity is ensured through a thorough description of the research framework. To assure an exact observation of reality, different data sources are used to triangulate the results. In

---

40 Construct validity is not relevant in this context as value chain architecture and bargaining structure are both concepts that are easy to understand.

addition to interviews conducted with practitioners, I screened secondary sources, such as publications, company internal documents and data bases, to confirm my results. Further, to get a comprehensive picture of the bargaining structure in place and of the reasons for developments and decisions, I interviewed practitioners from firms on different levels of the value chain, from OEM to tier-2 suppliers. On the other hand, I compare the tentative answers are compared with the observed patterns to further enhance internal validity.

Second, the small number of cases considered poses a challenge to external validity, that is, to the generalizability of results. Although the number of analyzed cases in this research project conflicts with the four to 10 recommended by Eisenhardt (1989), through the selection of representative cases, a thorough sampling process, and a detailed description of the context of each case I aim to facilitate cross-case analysis. Nevertheless, given the explorative nature of the research, the selected case studies are sufficient to indicate drivers of bargaining structures and show that instances exist in which bargaining structures change.

Last, the question of reliability in qualitative research is more problematic than in quantitative approaches. It is questionable whether case studies can be viewed as reliable since an interview is a one-time event with a special dynamic and, thus, not easily reproducible (Lamnek 1995). Nevertheless, following Gibbert et al. (2008) reliability is enhanced through a clear documentation of the research steps to enable replication of the study.

In the subsequent section, the research process is described following Yin (1984) and Eisenhardt (1989).

5.1.1 Case design

Two different case studies are used in the present research in order to achieve robust results and draw a precise picture. Similar to quantitative research methods, the selection of cases is critical to ensure generalizability. However, cases are not randomly selected, but are rather chosen for theoretical reasons (Glaser and Strauss 1967). A structured selection approach was followed to identify the most appropriate cases.

Every bargaining structure has a possible alternative structure that could serve to understand the drivers and actions that support the prevailing structure ("why this one and not any other one"). However, bargaining structures that have undergone changes are considered the most promising cases. As this research focuses on a shift from one bargaining structure to another, one can observe the actions of participants and see which levers they have applied instead of comparing the status quo to hypothetical alternatives.

However, bargaining structures of most value chains are not transparent to outsiders. Therefore, I developed a long list of potential cases using literature, experts, and practitioners drawn from different industries (see Table 17).

No.	Industry	Company	Product/Case	Change of bargaining structure	Source for first assessment
1	IT services	*Confidential*	IT outsourcing services	No	Industry expert
2	Commercial aircraft	Boeing, Airbus	B787, A350	Yes	Literature
3	Semiconductor	Intel	System on a chip	Yes	Practitioner
4	Automotive	confidential	Lighting system	Yes	Industry expert
5	Home appliances	Bosch Siemens Hausgeräte	Laundry dryer	Yes	Industry expert
6	Aerospace	*confidential*	Research cooperation	No	Practitioner
7	Elevator	Kone	Elevator design	No	Practitioner
8	Tractor	*Confidential*	Tractor	Yes	Industry expert

Table 17: Long list of potential research cases

In case study research, the selection of strongly contrasting cases facilitates the identification of general patterns and theory building (Eisenhardt 1989). Therefore I chose industries that are very different in nature—commercial aircraft (focusing on aircraft manufacturing at Boeing and Airbus) and home appliances (analyzing the laundry dryer value chain with Bosch Siemens Hausgeräte (BSH) as OEM). While the aircraft industry is characterized by long product cycles, low-volume products, high technological requirements, and a high degree of specialization of players, the home appliance market is a mass market with more or less standardized products. Detailed descriptions of the two cases chosen are set forth later in this chapter.

5.1.2 Data sources and analysis

Interviews, internal documents, publications, and data bases were used to achieve a full understanding of the cases. The present section provides an overview of the approaches used for each of the sources.

Case interviews

Case interviews are the primary data source used. In total, I engaged 11 practitioners in semi-structured interviews based on a questionnaire developed beforehand. The questionnaire was readjusted based on new findings over the course of the interview phase. While changes should not be made to a questionnaire during the data collection period in quantitative research projects, the adaptions are a key part of the applied method. Following Strauss and Corbin (1990) and Yin (1984), it is critical to incorporate findings from the first interviews into the questionnaire as the overall structure of the problem only becomes transparent over the course of the interviews. A final version of the questionnaire can be found in Appendix G. Because of the different contexts (home appliance and commercial aircraft) and roles of the interviewees (OEM, tier-1, and tier-2 suppliers), questionnaires were slightly different and not all questions were posed in every interview. Although it would have facilitated the evaluation, there was no strict adherence to the structure and sequence of questions so that interviewee's line of thought was not interrupted and possible unexpected findings could be uncovered. The set of guiding questions was sent to the interviewees via email two to five days prior to the scheduled interview to allow sufficient time for preparation.

In the case of BSH, a primary contact person at the company assisted in the development of a list of possible interviewees who had and active role in the design and production of the T20 laundry dryer. The interviewees were drawn from firms at different levels of the value chain, ranging from OEM to tier-2 suppliers to give a clear view on value chain and bargaining structure. For the aircraft case, I rely on interviews with former managers of OEMs (Boeing and Airbus) and a tier-2 supplier. The interviewees were identified through a search on the professional network LinkedIn and on personal recommendations. All interviewees have extensive experience with supplier interaction in the aircraft value chain. In addition, a rich set of secondary data—that is discussed later—is used to gain clear insights. An overview of the case interviews is provided in Table 18. Profiles of the interviewees can be found in Appendix H.

The interviews were conducted in the period of July 2014 to October 2014 over the telephone in the mother tongue of the interviewees, seven in German and the rest in English. The interviews took between 30 and 70 minutes with an average duration of 45 minutes and all interviews were recorded and transcribed. Interviews conducted in German were not translated into English in order to prevent any bias and the loss of information.

In the first step of the analysis, the interviews were summarized and text modules categorized according to a predefined coding scheme consisting of eight categories: context, product architecture, value chain architecture, bargaining structure, replaceability of firms, power to shape bargaining structure, levers applied, and reasons for shaping bargaining structure. The scheme served as a basic structure for the questionnaire as well.

Secondary data

A broad set of secondary sources enriches the database (Table 19 provides an overview). Besides the interview transcripts, the BSH case analysis is based on internal documents and a publication by Feldhusen et al. (2013). While the internal documents provide a picture of the changes in the value chain, the publication highlights how the new modular product architecture enables a broader product portfolio and drives the value chain architecture.

For the commercial aircraft case, a set of published articles and business school cases, as well as a database on aircraft suppliers, were considered for the case analysis. The case of the Boeing 787 has been widely used to discuss different managerial challenges, in particular, supplier management, supply chain risks and outsourcing decisions, (Elahi et al. 2014, Kotha et al. 2005, Shih 2014, Tang and Zimmermann 2010). The value chain architecture is a central part of many of the publications considered, with some indicating how the bargaining structure changed at the same time.

Case	Company	Position in value chain	Role of interviewee	Date
Home appliance – laundry dryer	BSH	OEM	Project Director T20	2014-07-03
Home appliance – laundry dryer	BSH	OEM	Vice President Purchasing	2014-07-08
Home appliance – laundry dryer	BSH	OEM	Project manager T20	2014-07-16
Home appliance – laundry dryer	Coko-Werk	Tier-1 supplier	Responsible sales and project manager T20	2014-07-18
Home appliance – laundry dryer	Wirthwein	Tier-1 supplier	Factory manager	2014-09-02
Home appliance – laundry dryer	Prettl/PAS	Tier-2 supplier	Head of Research & Development	2014-07-25
Commercial aircraft	Airbus	OEM	Head of strategic procurement for metal components	2014-08-01
Commercial aircraft	Airbus	OEM	Senior Vice President Procurement Strategy	2014-10-06
Commercial aircraft	Boeing	OEM	Executive Vice President	2014-10-02
Commercial aircraft	Boeing	OEM	Vice President Engineering	2014-10-02
Commercial aircraft	HITCO Carbon Composites; Boeing	Tier-2 supplier; OEM	Executive Vice President; Senior Contract Manager and Senior Business Manager	2014-10-13

Table 18: List of interviewees

Case	Type	Source	Information
Home appliance – laundry dryer	Internal document	BSH	Overview of product and value chain architecture
	Internal document	BSH	T20 project overview, presented on 14 October 2014 in Munich
	Publication	Feldhusen et al. 2013	Discussion of modular product architecture to enable variety
Commercial aircraft	Database	Airframer (2014)	Suppliers by aircraft program
	Publication	Airbus (2014)	Airbus approved supplier list
	Publication	Boeing (2009)	Boeing quality management system requirements for suppliers
	Publication	Cassiolato et al. (2002)	Case study of Embraer in Brazil
	Publication	Tang and Zimmermann (2010)	Overview of change in value chain architecture, financial setup with tier-1 suppliers
	Publication	Kotha and Srikanth (2013)	Case background, overview of value chain architecture, reasons for modularization and value chain changes
	Publication	Elahi et al. (2014)	Overview value chain architecture, discussion of reasons for value chain changes
	Business School Case	Kotha et al. (2005)	Case background, market perspective, value chain
	Business School Case	Shih (2014)	Case background, reasons for value chain changes

Table 19: Secondary data sources

High-level categories of products of aerospace suppliers	
Airframe Systems	Design
Avionics	Management
Components	Production
Materials	Testing
Power Systems	

Table 20: Airframer product categories

On the other side, the Airframer (2014) database is used to understand the replaceability of firms involved in the aircraft production. Airframer is a comprehensive database providing information on aircraft programs, manufacturers, and suppliers. It lists 1,152 aircrafts in the commercial, business, sport, and military segment, and 4,478 suppliers. For every aircraft program, Airframer provides a list of suppliers by category (see Table 20), subcategory, and country. Suppliers offering various products are listed in all respective categories.

I use a three-step approach to identify suppliers that are hard to replace in the value chain. First, data on large passenger aircraft programs is analyzed to identify suppliers that are involved in a product subcategory for almost all programs. The analysis includes only large passenger aircraft programs of Boeing and Airbus in order to achieve high comparability with the two aircraft programs chosen for the case study, those of the B787 and the A350. The relevant dataset consists of 2,214 products and 736 suppliers participating in one or more of the following aircraft programs: Boeing 747, 767, 777, 787; Airbus A330, A350, A380. I identified 78 suppliers covering 89 product subcategories that are involved in at least five of seven relevant aircraft programs. Thereof, 38 suppliers active in 46 product subcategories are involved in at least six of seven aircraft programs.

Second, I analyzed and compared the description of products provided by Airframer all aircraft programs to understand if an identified firm supplies a single product to (instead of different products in the same subcategory). Thus, suppliers such as C & D Zodiac, a firm that is listed for all large passenger aircraft programs as a supplier of cabin interiors, but which provides different products in different aircraft programs (lavatory equipment, window reveals, door surrounds, cabin stairs, storage bins), were removed from the initial list. In total, 60 firms with 66 products are involved in at least five aircraft programs, and, of these, 30 firms provide 35 products to at least six aircraft programs.

Third, to understand the competitive situation of each firm in the respective product market, the Airframer database and the Internet were searched for companies that supply similar products to one of the aircraft programs ensuring that none of the identified suppliers face a dual sourcing strategy of their downstream partner.[41] Hence, a list of 10 suppliers (with 11 products) that can be seen as nearly essential is developed (see Table 21).

5.2 Results of the case studies

In the present section, each of the cases will be analyzed to understand the determinants of bargaining structure, the interplay of value chain architecture and bargaining structure, and to gain an understanding of the applicability and effects of the hierarchy strategy in real-world settings. The cases of the aircraft and laundry dryer value chains will show that value chain architecture mostly coincides with bargaining structure and is a key determinant. Further, firms that are hard to replace can directly shape the bargaining structure. Although the cases differ with regard to the characteristics of the industry and the replaceability of firms, the observed determinants of bargaining structure are the same. In both cases, firms do not consider bargaining structure itself as a lever to enhance value capture, but rather that they directly or indirectly influence it to create or strengthen a bottleneck position; thus, firms do not capture the full potential with regard to the hierarchy strategy.

Following, each case will be discussed separately. After an introduction to the context of the case and challenges that stimulated change, the value chain architecture and drivers of its change will be illustrated. I will analyze to what extent the value chain architecture coincides with and drives the bargaining structure. From instances in which the two structures differ from each other, further drivers of bargaining structure are

---

41 Dual or multiple sourcing of a component is a common means used by firms to increase replaceability of their suppliers; as can be seen in the automotive sector (Ro et al. 2008; Jacobides and MacDuffie 2013).

identified. Further, to determine the effects of the changes in bargaining structure, the replaceability of firms in the value chain is analyzed. For each case, model-theoretic implications, that is, who benefits and loses from the changes, are discussed. Last, other effects of the change in value chain architecture will be shown in order to understand further consequences on value generation and capture (with regard to bottleneck) and reasons that drive firms' actions.

5.2.1. Modularization of laundry dryers at BSH

BSH is, with a revenue of more than 10bn Euro, one of the largest producers of home appliances selling laundry dryers and other products to consumers (Bosch Siemens Hausgeräte GmbH 2014). In 2005, the laundry dryer business unit initiated a project to gain a competitive edge. It was hoped the project would help manage the balancing act of increased complexity resulting from a larger variety of products and the need to reduce costs. At the same time, there was a push to focus on BSH's core competencies, which were seen in the business segment of laundry products as cleaning and drying. That is, non-core activities such as the development of electronics should no longer be fulfilled by BSH, but rather given to suppliers.

The answer to these issues was the T20—a new and highly modular laundry dryer. At the center of the new product architecture was a standardized base-module that was used for all versions in the BSH family of laundry dryers and could be produced efficiently. It contained the floor assembly and core technology of the laundry dryer. In

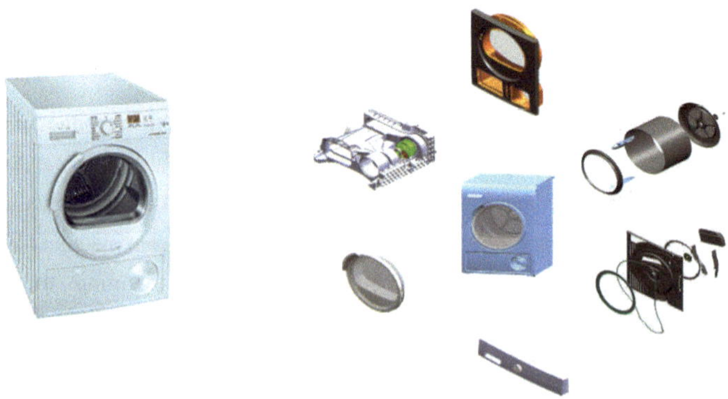

Figure 14: Laundry dryer T20 (left) and core systems (right) (Bosch Siemens Hausgeräte GmbH 2014)

addition, the product architecture consisted of five other systems: front, drum, back board, control panel, and door module. Further, there were a small number of components, such as the side walls. See Figure 14 and Figure 15 for an overview of the product architecture.

Product architecture mirrors value chain architecture

The change in product architecture went hand-in-hand with a change in the value chain architecture. With the design of independent systems, BSH introduced system suppliers to take over responsibility for the development and production of these parts. In particular, these suppliers performed the integration of the systems, a task mostly done by BSH beforehand.[42]

While the drum and the back board remained with BSH, three system suppliers produced the other parts. For the base and front module, one of the former suppliers of components in this field, the firm Wirthwein, was chosen by BSH as system supplier. While it only supplied selected components to the preceding model, the T10, it took over responsibility for up to 54 components, the respective suppliers, and the integration. Hence, according to the responsible factory manager Wirthwein already preassembled between 50-65% of the overall laundry dryer. Similarly, Coko-Werk took over responsibility for producing the door-module and E.G.O. Blanc und Fischer & Co. (E.G.O.) for producing the control panel.

Further, through the establishment of system suppliers, a number of firms moved from tier-1 to tier-2 suppliers in the value chain. These firms, which were used to deliver their products directly to BSH, became suppliers of the respective system suppliers for the T20 project. Thus, the total number of direct suppliers was significantly reduced in comparison to the previous version, the T10, from 68 to less than 20.

---

[42] The share of pre-assembled parts in BSH's final assembly differed by region and factory. In most cases, for example, in the Berlin factory, there was no pre-assembly of components. In some cases, either component suppliers or pure integrators did pre-assemble some components.

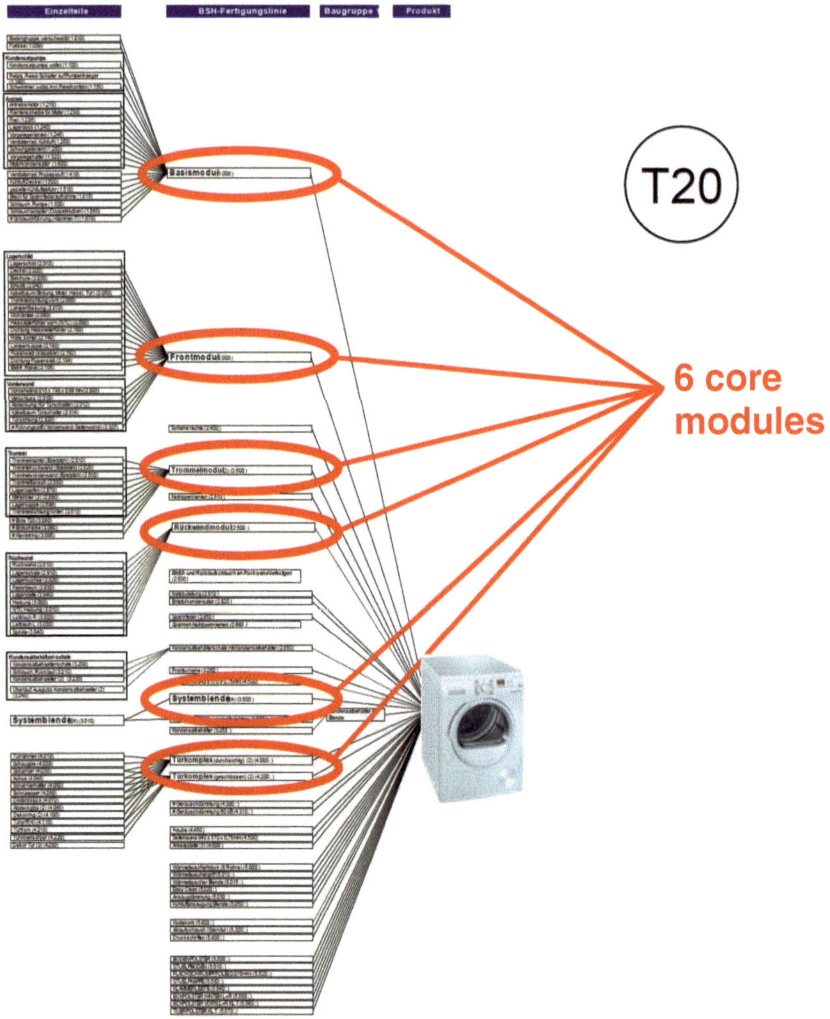

Figure 15: Product architecture of the laundry dryer T20 (Bosch Siemens Hausgeräte GmbH 2014)

BSH had the full power to redesign the product and value chain architecture, as the following quotes show:

> *"Based on the pre-condition of a short final assembly line and delivery of systems, we designed the product architecture of the laundry dryer. [...] Based on this, we were able to decide how to split the work among suppliers."*
> *(Jungerberg, Project Director T20 at BSH)*

> *"The functionality of the system was given by BSH. The physical interfaces to other systems [...] were as well specified by BSH. For the detailed design of the door system, BSH initiated a concept competition."*
> *(Lange, Responsible sales and project manager T20 at Coko-Werk)*

BSH not only defined the boundaries of modules and thus the product architecture on the highest level but also the architecture of the value chain through setting the functional requirements of systems and designing the interfaces. Moreover, BSH shaped the product architecture of systems through concept competitions among potential system suppliers as well.

Bargaining structure driven by value chain architecture and individual firms

The interview results show that for most parts the bargaining structure coincided and changed in parallel with the value chain architecture. Hence, the value chain architecture, and, in turn, the product architecture, was a key driver of the bargaining structure. For example, as E.G.O. became the system supplier for the system control panel[43] it took over responsibility of managing the tier-2 suppliers. Among them was Prettl,[44] which delivered plastic parts, tooling equipment, and wiring harnesses for the system control panel of the T20. Prettl was once a direct supplier to BSH, but for the T20, Prettl negotiated prices and volumes with E.G.O. and had almost no interaction with BSH. Thus, the change in product architecture that BSH performed entailed corresponding changes in both the value chain architecture and the bargaining structure.

---

43 An important reason for selecting E.G.O. for the system supplier role was its experience in electronics, in particular with touch-technology. In the selection process it was the only one to offer a system control panel with touch pads instead of mechanical buttons.

44 Today the company is named PAS Deutschland GmbH, part of the Prettl Produktions Holding GmbH.

In some instances, however, the bargaining structure deviated from the value chain architecture. The following examples show that these differences were caused by the action of two firms with strong positions in the value chain, that is, firms that are hard to replace. Obviously, these firms actively manage the bargaining structure.

First, BSH decided to keep responsibility for the procurement of selected components regardless of the position of the respective supplier in the value chain. The tier-2 components directly negotiated by BSH had one of the following two characteristics: either BSH could realize a higher volume effect by purchasing them directly, or the components were crucial for differentiating features of the product, as the following statements show:

> *"We don't want to lose our core lever—the bundling of volume."*
> *(Vice President Purchasing at BSH)*

> *"There are some parts and basic materials that are preset by our customer. [...] These are key components, for example, displays and electronics, for which prices are directly negotiated by the customer."*
> *(Seikel, Director of R&D at Prettl)*

For example, BSH managed the procurement of specific granulate material. The granulate creates the characteristic white color that is associated with BSH home appliances and not only is used in several systems and components of tier-1 and tier-2 suppliers but also in all other home appliance products produced. Thus, BSH can achieve a lower purchase price by bundling the volume for all products instead of handing over responsibility to the respective system or component suppliers. While system suppliers still managed the supply of these components, and even negotiated contract details such as terms of payment, delivery date, and financing, price negotiations remained with BSH. The following statement from a system supplier shows the split of responsibilities:

> *"[For these components] we controlled the quantity balance, disposal, orders, logistics, and quality. [...] We were responsible for negotiating technical and design issues in the development process, and liabilities for defects—not the price. [...] BSH orders the product from a supplier X with quantity Y. From that quantity we can buy the components at a fixed price, negotiated by BSH."*
> *(Sauerwald, factory manager at Wirthwein)*

A similar example is the window glass used in the door system. As BSH could bundle the volume required for dryer and laundry machines, the management decided to negotiate prices and volumes directly with the supplier Arc International and omit the system supplier Coko-Werk. Further, BSH kept control over components that were critical for the functionality and differentiation of its products. For example, after the T20 project, Prettl became system supplier of the system control panel and electronics were supplied by a new tier-2 supplier. As BSH perceived electronics as a core differentiating feature of its products, it wanted to be involved in the development and took over the procurement of these parts.

Second, the tier-2 window glass supplier, Arc International, pushed for direct negotiations with BSH. It would accept only BSH as its bargaining counterpart. Although the system supplier, Coko-Werk, was present in some of the negotiations and the direct recipient of the window glasses, Arc International approached BSH for day-to-day management issues such as quality complaints from Coko-Werk.

Replaceability of firms

BSH and Arc International have a common trait. They both have a very strong position in the value chain and are nearly non-replaceable. BSH, in its role as the OEM, had some unique assets and capabilities such as its brand and customer access, the size of the customer base, explicit and tacit knowledge on the product design and production process, and the know-how of managing a large group of suppliers. Furthermore, although system suppliers could gain an advantage through the newly acquired capabilities of being the integrator, for most of them BSH represented a significant share of their revenues. Thus, they faced a kind of lock-in and were in a relatively weak position compared with BSH. Similarly, Arc International was in a dominant position as it was the only producer that was able to offer the window glass for a competitive price. At the same time, the laundry dryer business represented only a minor part of the overall business, which increased Arc International's bargaining power. These findings suggest that the strong positions of BSH and Arc International allowed them to directly shape the bargaining structure, deviating from the value chain architecture.

Model-theoretic implications

Although the interviewees indicated that neither the bargaining structure per se was the reason for change, nor did it play a role during modularization of the product, the results from sections 4.2 and 4.3 suggest that BSH could benefit with regard to value capture from the hierarchical bargaining structure. The situation can be modeled as a bargaining structure with two essential firms, BSH and Arc International. As discussed above, each has unique capabilities and assets that make them nearly non-replaceable. All other firms, including system suppliers, can be seen as relatively non-essential.

After the introduction of system suppliers, BSH bargained with a smaller number of relatively non-essential direct system suppliers instead of a large number of component suppliers. As BSH's assets, such as customer access and reputation, only come into play for the final product, it can be assumed that complementarity is largest in the final integration step. Hence, the model results in Section 4.2.2 and 4.3.1 predict that the new bargaining structure had a positive effect on BSH's value capture.

On the supplier side, there are winners and losers of the change. First, the model indicates that Arc International could benefit from the increased hierarchy. Because of its strong position in top-level negotiations, benefits gained by BSH through the consolidation of suppliers are presumably shared with Arc International. In particular, the push of Arc International to keep its position in top-level negotiations and directly negotiate with BSH is in line with the hierarchy strategy.

Further, for firms that were moved to a lower level in the bargaining structure, the change was disadvantageous from a bargaining and value capture perspective. Based on the results from Section 4.2.2 and 4.3.1, these firms most probably lose from the new bargaining structure with regard to the hierarchy strategy.

Last, for suppliers that became system suppliers whether they could benefit from the new bargaining structure mainly depends on their ability to decrease replaceability. If they cannot gain a stronger position, generate a lock-in effect for BSH, thus, decreasing the risk of being replaced, the new bargaining structure is most likely disadvantageous. As discussed in Section 4.3.1 although they take over the integrator role, they might have lost from the new structure.

Further effects of changes in the value chain architecture, beyond bargaining structure

The changes in the value chain had significant effects on BSH and the system suppliers. BSH, on the one side, was able to reduce its own value creation activities as the system suppliers assembled the systems and delivered integrated products to it. Hence, BSH could focus on the final integration step and the production of the base-module. Further, in the new structure, the system producers were the ones to enable the variation of the product through variations in their respective systems. This allowed BSH to offer a large portfolio of laundry dryers to customers with only little additional complexity as production did not require variation of the overall design. This was a driving factor for the compilation of modules into systems. BSH achieved a reduction of complexity and gained a positive financial effect through a shortened production lead time.

On the other side, though system suppliers faced new challenges, some of them improved their standing in the value chain. Most system suppliers had already supplied components for previous versions of the laundry dryer. However, the new role required new capabilities. Coko-Werk, the system supplier for the door system, had supplied large injection molded parts for the T10. It now needed to acquire new skills for the assembly technology as well as knowledge on new components to be produced and sourced from their new suppliers. Although BSH would have been able to reincorporate the integration activities, a few system suppliers could slightly increase switching costs through the newly acquired capabilities and production setup.[45] Hence, they could strengthen the ties with BSH and gain a positive effect.

5.2.2. System suppliers in commercial aircraft manufacturing

The supply, or value chain, of a large passenger aircraft is complex. A typical aircraft consists of six million parts, around 85% of the cost of an aircraft is procured, and interdependencies exist between many systems that must be considered during design and production. Further, a new aircraft requires heavy investments, in particular by the OEM, and delays can become costly. Hence, the management of the value chain is the highest priority for aircraft manufacturers. In the last decade, there have been significant structural changes in aircraft value chains. As the interviews showed, both Airbus and Boeing introduced an additional level to their tiered supplier structure. Large system suppliers, so called mega suppliers, took over production of major sections of the aircraft and ship fully integrated parts, for example, the nose section or the wings, to the OEMs. This trend[46] started in the mid-1990's with Embraer being one of the first aircraft manufacturers to shift workload and parts of the integration process to selected

---

[45] Many system producers located their factories close to BSH's final assembly line.

[46] Apart from the specific aircraft programs mentioned, interview results confirmed that the introduction of mega suppliers can be seen as a general trend in aircraft manufacturing.

suppliers. The most prominent recent examples are the Airbus A350 and the Boeing 787 Dreamliner aircraft programs.

Traditionally, aircraft OEMs were the key manufacturers and assemblers of the overall aircraft as well as of its subsystems. In order to control the overall design, suppliers were given detailed instructions on how to build components—a so-called build to print approach. The components produced by suppliers were then shipped to the OEM, which integrated them into subsystems and assembled the aircraft.

As practitioners from Boeing and Airbus indicated, this approach caused tremendous administrative costs for OEMs as they were orchestrating thousands of suppliers. Besides the management of suppliers, it required a huge effort of procurement and quality control units to ensure that the OEM received a certain component at the right time, quality, and price to assemble the aircraft. In some cases, OEMs were just intermediaries between suppliers. They bought parts from one supplier to ship it to another supplier who would build it into its system. For example, Boeing had more than 33,000 direct suppliers in the year 2000 (including aerospace and defense suppliers), a number that suggests huge complexity and a large cost base.

At the same time, OEMs needed to invest heavily in the development of an aircraft. The build to print approach required detailed instruction for every component, which significantly drove engineering costs. Further, long final assembly time at the OEM plant caused low turnover and high inventory cost—which all led to bad financial results.

Changing value chain architecture

Aircraft OEMs tried to tackle these problems by directly changing value chain architecture and introducing new tier-1 suppliers. Mega suppliers are typically former direct suppliers of components or small systems to the OEM that take over responsibility for designing and producing large sections of the aircraft. They not only deliver integrated sections to the OEM but also manage the supply chain for their respective system. Supplier relations, which were once with the OEM, are taken over by the system supplier, thus, changing the value chain architecture to a more hierarchical form.

For the 787 Dreamliner, Boeing established a global partnership model empowering 12 selected suppliers with control and ownership of large modules of the aircraft that could be built independently (see Figure 16). One of them, Kawasaki, was chosen as a tier-1 supplier for one of the fuselage sections.

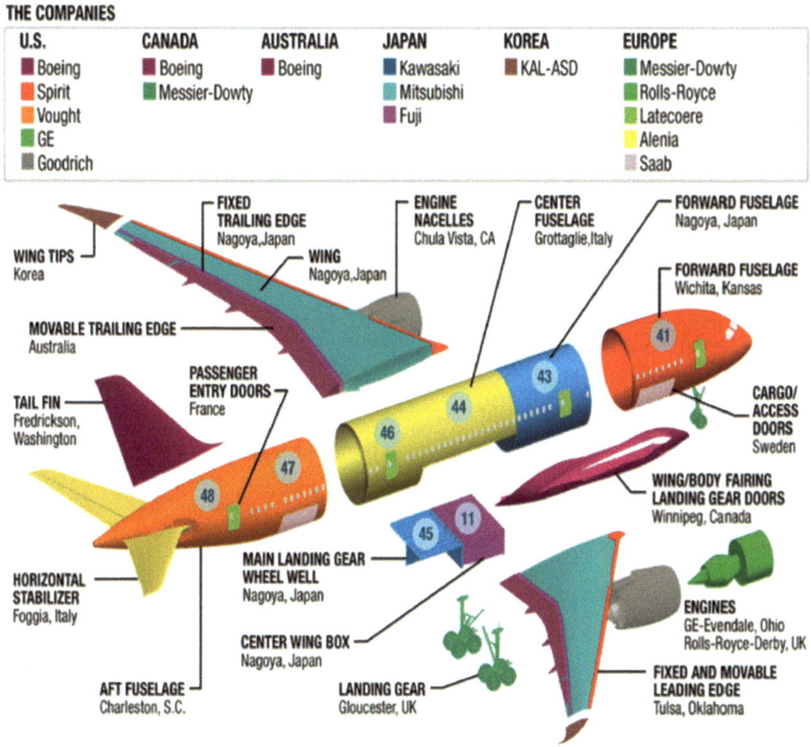

Figure 16: List of Boeing's tier-1 suppliers and top-level modules for the 787(Kotha and Nolan 2005)

> *"When the barrel section of a fuselage gets in, all the wiring, hydraulic lines, floor beams, and side walls are in it. It is as close to a finished product as it can possibly be. It used to be different in the past."*
> *(Former Executive Vice President at Boeing)*

As mentioned, mega suppliers not only assemble the assigned section but also take over responsibility for managing the supply chain. Hence, Kawasaki has to select and manage the suppliers of side walls, floor beams wires, hydraulic lines, and floor beams. These suppliers have become tier-2 suppliers in contrast to former aircraft programs in which they directly supplied to Boeing. Similarly, Mitsubishi producing the wings buys fuel pumps from a tier-2 supplier and integrates them into the wing. Formerly, Boeing would have bought the fuel pumps separately and would have integrated them into the wing itself. Through the delivery of integrated assemblies, Boeing could reduce the final assembly time of the 787 to three days. In addition, instances in which OEMs were just intermediaries were eliminated. Tier-2 suppliers went directly to tier-1s, and tier-3 suppliers went to tier-2s.

OEMs are the driving force behind the changes in the value chain architecture, as a former Boeing manager assures:

> *"They [OEMs] enforced them [suppliers], pushed them, encouraged them—whatever word you want to use—to readjust to the new tier structure."*
> *(Former Executive Vice President at Boeing)*

In this context, product architecture played only a minor role. Apart from minor changes, mostly in the area of interfaces,[47] value chain architecture was shaped without significantly changing product architecture. However, these shifts were rather consequences of than drivers of the changes in the value chain.

Bargaining structure driven by value chain architecture and OEMs

The results show that the bargaining structure mostly changed in parallel to the value chain architecture. In only a few cases did bargaining structure deviate as OEMs directly influenced it.

Besides the new tasks and responsibilities,[48] mega suppliers gained additional degrees of freedom as they faced less interference of the OEM in their operations. As they have full responsibility for the value chain of their respective aircraft section, they have the freedom to select lower tier suppliers themselves[49] and run negotiations with

---

47 Successful final integration by the OEM requires the definition of precise interfaces between the large aircraft sections. This is a result of the transfer of production and integration activities to tier-1 suppliers.

48 In some cases, the risk sharing structure and new responsibilities of mega suppliers caused serious problems in the supply chain. Interview results and publications show that, in particular, the inconsistent management of risks among mega suppliers, capabilities gaps with regard to the new complex design and integration tasks, and the high upfront investments (for R&D, prototypes, etc.) that pushed some suppliers close to or into illiquidity are the main issues arising from the new approach.

49 OEMs set requirements that lower tier suppliers need to fulfill to ensure technical capabilities and mitigate risks. Nevertheless, the decision of which firm is selected as supplier for a tier-2 component is, in most cases, with the mega supplier.

them independently. Thus, the changes in the value chain architecture, which introduced an additional layer in the tiered structure, had an impact as well on the bargaining structure. As only a few mega suppliers were introduced, a large number of former tier-1 suppliers were moved to tier-2, now negotiating with the mega supplier responsible for the focal aircraft section instead of bargaining with the OEM. Hence, the bargaining structure changed from almost non-hierarchical to a hierarchical form.

For example, for the Airbus A350, Spirit AeroSystems has taken over the design and production of the center fuselage section from Airbus. While Airbus once directly purchased components and subsystems for other aircraft programs to install in the fuselage—such as the oxygen system—Spirit AeroSystems now manages and directly negotiates with these suppliers for the A350 program. Similarly, Triumph, the supplier of doors for the 787, and Nordam, the supplier of floor panels, have moved to tier-2 and negotiate with the respective mega suppliers.

In general, the changes in the value chain architecture implied changes in the bargaining structure, which is not surprising given the OEMs' goal to reduce administrative costs. A former Senior Vice President of Procurement Strategy puts the new approach in the following way:

> *"We negotiate at system level, not component level."*
> *(Andrew, former Senior Vice President Procurement Strategy at Airbus)*

At the same time, there are two further reasons why OEMs leave negotiations with lower tier suppliers to mega suppliers. First, as mega suppliers often supply several OEMs with similar products (e.g., Spirit AeroSystems provides fuselage sections both to Boeing and Airbus) they can bundle purchasing volume and are likely to garner better prices. Second, OEMs do not interfere in negotiations between mega and lower tier suppliers as they might become liable in case of technical difficulties with the respective system.

However, there are instances driven by the OEMs in which value chain architecture and bargaining structure do not coincide. For certain commodities, in particular raw materials such as titanium, aluminum-lithium, and carbon fiber, OEMs negotiate enablement contracts with the respective tier-4 suppliers to ensure competitiveness through a low guaranteed price and secure the required capacity. The OEM can realize higher volume effects than any of its suppliers through bundling the demand for 120,000 pounds of titanium per aircraft. At the same time, in case of supply shortages (in particular during the ramp-up phase), the OEM has control over the allocation of input materials and can prioritize components that are the most critical to the project.

Suppliers are free to tap into the volume negotiated by the OEM, but may use other sources as well. Hence, for raw materials, contract structure for the most part does not coincide with bargaining structure as suppliers enter into an agreement with the raw material supplier without negotiating the price. Likewise, OEMs seek to control a few selected critical suppliers to mitigate technical risks and costs. For example, Boeing still directly interacts with Rockwell Collins, formally a tier-2 supplier of avionics that are pre-installed in the nose section of the aircraft. The navigation system and auto-pilot that Rockwell Collins supplies are of high technical risk, as the systems are, to a large extent, interconnected with other parts of the aircraft.[50] Because of the number of interfaces to other suppliers that need to be managed, Boeing wants to be involved in order to control the risk of problems and delays. Therefore, Rockwell Collins has remained a direct supplier of Boeing.

In addition, the interviews revealed that OEMs take advantage of negotiations on a group level if several direct suppliers are part of a conglomerate. Hence, multiple top-level bargaining positions result in a single integrated position.

> *"To give an example one major supplier to Airbus has about 20 companies in the group. Within those 20 companies you have a variety of products from hydraulic equipment, to complete systems including Aerostructures. What this allows Airbus and the Supplier to do is use the magnitude of the overall business to be flexible in areas such as pricing anomalies, technical support and future investments by working at group level with the CEO and his team as opposed to business unit level."*
> *(Andrew, former Senior Vice President Procurement Strategy at Airbus)*

Replaceability of firms

Overall, beyond the OEMs, a large number of the firms in the aircraft value chain can be considered as nearly essential. OEMs have a strong standing in the value chain because of their integration capabilities, project management skills, supplier relationships, and customer access. The high level of essentiality in the supplier base is due to the following three reasons that will be discussed in detail: little competition in

50 The systems require, for example, input from the flight control system and the fuel quantity system (to know the balance and weight of the aircraft).

many component and system markets, high switching costs, and customer appreciation of consistency in the supplier base.

First, many component and system markets are dominated by a few specialist firms because of technical, administrative, and logistic requirements.

> *"For complex systems, only few technical specialists persist and there is very limited competition, as it can be observed, for example, for aircraft doors. [...] Further, there are enormous logistic requirements. This does not only hold for high-tech components but also for trivial parts. [...] An additional key reason for so many suppliers being difficult to replace are the certification requirements." (Von Zitzewitz, former head of strategic procurement for metal components at Airbus)*

Many parts are complex and require specialized capabilities for design and production. The step toward "build to performance" even increases the capability requirements for some suppliers as they take over the design and integration activities. For example, the landing flaps are complex, not only from a mechanical perspective but also from an integration perspective. Hence, suppliers need to have specialized knowledge to design the interfaces (hydraulic and electric connections). In addition, for most components and systems there are no alternative designs available or implementable at reasonable cost, which could foster competition.

Further, suppliers need to comply with aerospace standards (e.g., AS9100) and be certified and approved by the OEM. They must have a very sophisticated documentation process installed in order to clarify liability in case of problems or accidents. At the same time, suppliers face high logistic requirements. OEMs want to have transparency on the status of production for single components and systems in order to ensure on-time delivery and to identify potential issues early. As a single missing component can stop the final assembly and cause tremendous costs, OEMs demand the implementations of IT systems from suppliers to monitor the supply chain. As an example, cross beams are built into the fuselage for stabilization and carry the floor plates. Every cross beam is customized depending on its position in the aircraft, the configuration of the cabin interior, and the electric configuration of the aircraft. Despite the rather low technical complexity, it requires intensive interaction between the mega supplier and the supplier of cross beams, connected IT systems, and a sophisticated process to have the right beam at the assembly of the fuselage section at the right time. Currently, there are only two suppliers that are capable of producing the cross beams for large passenger aircraft.

Second, switching costs are high due to the interdependency of systems. For example, landing gears are tightly integrated into the aircraft. In order to change the supplier, one would have to significantly alter the overall design of the aircraft as the landing gear is a proprietary part. This would involve a major engineering effort for which the OEM might not have the capacity.

OEMs are generally loyal with respect to their suppliers as they fear the complexity and risk involved in switching, particularly in cases of introducing a new supplier to the value chain. As issues and delays in a single component can have tremendous effects on the overall program performance, OEMs stick to the suppliers that have proven to be reliable and trustworthy.

Third, airlines appreciate consistency in the supplier base. Having different suppliers for the same component adds maintenance costs and complexity. Therefore, airlines want to have a single supplier for a given part for all aircrafts of the same type and ideally even across their fleet. Thus, a switch in suppliers might hurt customer relationships and affect sales of the OEM.

All these aspects put supplier into a rather strong position, particularly after the start of an aircraft program. As the required design changes resulting from a switch of a single supplier would set back and delay the program for months, aircraft OEMs stick to their suppliers as long as possible.

> *"Switching suppliers is always the last choice."*
> *(Andrew, former Senior Vice President Procurement Strategy at Airbus)*

> *"Once you are on an airplane, you will probably be the supplier for the set of components you have been awarded for the entire life of the aircraft."*
> *(Former Executive Vice President at Boeing)*

Even in cases that endanger the success of the program, for example, if there are severe quality issues or if a supplier liquidates, aircraft OEMs are hesitant to replace suppliers. As a former manager of a tier-2 supplier reports, acquisition of suppliers in trouble by "friends" of the OEM along with changes in the management team to put them back on track is a typical approach to solve problems along the value chain.

> *"As a result [of severe problems]—that is what large OEMs do—they go to their friends and either have them compete[51] or they have them directly acquire the company they have problems with."*
> *(Carson, former Executive Vice President at HITCO Carbon Composites, former Senior Contract and Business Manager at Boeing)*

As indicated, supplier contracts are often awarded for the lifespan of an aircraft. In many cases, the development of components is still ongoing while the first prototypes are assembled. Although downstream firms (OEMs and mega suppliers) try to include potential upcoming requests (for changes or extra versions of a product)[52] in the base contract, it often triggers additional price negotiations during the design and ramp-up phase. For example, change requests from the airline that come in at a later stage of the development and concern the configuration of the cabin interior might imply changes to the floor beams and cause additional negotiations. However, at that point in time, switching costs are extremely high, which puts suppliers into a rather strong position.

All in all, interview results indicate that many suppliers can be considered nearly essential in negotiations along the aircraft value chain. The analysis of the Airframer supplier database presented in Section 5.1 (Airframer 2014) supports the results showing that there is a large number of suppliers that are in a monopoly-like position and nearly essential.

From the database of aircraft suppliers, I identified 60 firms that contribute 66 products to at least five of the seven large, commercial passenger aircraft programs of Airbus and Boeing.[53] Thereof, 46 products and 38 suppliers are involved in six or more aircraft programs. Being involved in almost all aircraft programs with the same product shows that the focal firm has a strong standing in the value chain and replacing it may come at a high cost.

---

51 Note that competition is a rather mid- or long-term oriented option and mostly not applicable within an ongoing aircraft program.

52 For example, a mega supplier or OEM might require an additional preliminary version of a component for testing the system.

53 The considered aircraft programs include Boeing 747, 767, 777, 787, Airbus A330, A350 WBX, and A380. Overall, the database lists 2,214 products and 736 suppliers that are involved in these programs.

Further, for 10 firms (with 11 products) supplying at least to six of the seven aircraft programs, there are no other firms supplying the same or similar products (see Table 21)—which suggests that these firms are potentially nearly essential.

Firm	**Product segment**	**Product(s)**
Dunmore	Materials / Non-metal Materials	Laminates: Interior surfacing films
General Ecology Inc.	Airframe Systems / Environmental Systems	Water Purification Systems
HR Smith (Technical Developments) Ltd	Components / Electrical Components	Static Dischargers
Kahn Industries Inc./Kahn & Co	Production / Measurement	Dynamometers
Latrobe Speciality Steel Company	Materials / Metals	Steel: High purity vacuum re-melted steel
M. Torres Disenos Industriales S.A.	Production / Machining	Milling systems with flexible tooling
M. Torres Disenos Industriales S.A.	Production / Tooling	Laser Tooling: Laser scribers with flexible tooling
Quantum Composites, Inc.	Materials / Composites	Reinforced Composite Molding Compounds: Epoxy/phenolic materials
Rockwell Collins Inc.	Avionics / Navigation Aids (Airborne)	Distance Measuring Equipment; Automatic Direction Finders
Testek, Inc.	Testing / Test Equipment	Generator test stand (variable frequency generator); Fuel test stand; Automatic test equipment test stand; Hydraulic test stand
Thales Avionics S.A.	Avionics / Indicators and Instruments	Electronic Flight Instrument Systems: Integrated Electronic Standby Instrument

Table 21: Nearly essential suppliers according to Airframer analysis

The results of the Airframer database can be considered a strong indicator that there are many firms in the aircraft supply chain that are hard to replace, although the outside-in view is not fully comprehensive. On the one side, the list of competitors among suppliers in the large passenger aircraft segment is not comprehensive as Airframer provides contracted suppliers but not any other tendering firms for a certain product. Thus, the identified firms may not be fully essential but may face replaceability at a certain cost (e.g., switching cist, reduced performance, customer satisfaction, or increased component costs). On the other side, the risk of firms that supply other aircraft programs (e.g., small passenger or military aircrafts) entering the segment of large passenger aircrafts cannot be assessed. However, in combination with the interview results, many suppliers can be considered hard to replace in the aircraft value chain and hence as nearly essential in negotiations.

Model-theoretic implications

The results from Sections 4.2.1 and 4.2.2 indicate that the new value chain architecture and bargaining structure have a positive effect on the value capture of OEMs. While many nearly essential firms are moved to tier-2, the OEMs keep their top-level positions in the new hierarchical bargaining structure.

In detail, according to Proposition 3, OEMs benefit from the changes in the bargaining structure as mega suppliers integrate the bargaining positions of many (nearly) essential suppliers. For example, B/E Aerospace supplies oxygen systems both to the Airbus A350 and to the Boeing 787. The oxygen system is a critical component to the fuselage sections managed by Spirit AeroSystems.[54] It is a very specialized component with only two capable suppliers on the market. As the production is complex (requiring clean rooms) and certification requirements are high, no alternative suppliers can easily enter the market. At the same time, high switching costs and potentially additional price negotiations during the development and ramp-up phase of the aircraft, when there is already a lock-in of suppliers, drives essentiality in the value distribution process. In the past, B/E Aerospace used to be a tier-1 supplier and oxygen systems would have been directly shipped to the OEM. According to the model results, the new position in the bargaining structure hurts the value capture of B/E Aerospace, but at the same time is

[54] Spirit AeroSystems supplies the center fuselages section to the Airbus A350 and the forward fuselage section to the Boeing 787.

beneficial for Boeing and Airbus. Similarly, interview results indicate that the producer of floor panels (Nordam) and doors (Triumph) are hard to replace in the value chain. Both were as well moved to tier-2 with the introduction of mega suppliers.

Further, the creation of mega suppliers also has an impact on groups of firms contributing diverse products to the aircraft, and, hence on the effect of mergers and acquisitions. In former cases in which the OEMs had a very large number of direct negotiation partners, having several inputs that were negotiated on the top-level with the OEM did not provide additional benefits to the supplier as bargaining positions could not be kept separate. OEMs initiated negotiations at group level, hence, consolidating potentially essential bargaining positions of the firms in the group. Through the introduction of tier-1 suppliers and the resulting hierarchical bargaining structure, groups of firms that, due to a diverse range of products supply to several mega suppliers, can keep bargaining positions separate and thus benefit with regard to value capture. Consequently, the acquisition of an additional firm and its bargaining position has become more beneficial if the firm is part of a different cluster, that is, it supplies to a different mega supplier.

For example, United Technologies Corporation has a broad portfolio of products, providing, among others, fuel systems, engine components, interior lighting systems, seating, parts of landing gear, and electrical power systems. While once a tier-1 supplier directly negotiating with Boeing, they are now a tier-2 supplier to different mega suppliers. The responsibility of mega suppliers for negotiations allows them to keep their bargaining positions separate and thus presumably increase value capture.

Further effects of changes in the value chain architecture, beyond bargaining structure

The changes in the value chain should help OEMs improve their financial returns. Mega suppliers are risk sharing partners, that is, they invest their own money for development and production of the systems and are rewarded when the aircraft is sold and shipped to the customer. Hence, the OEM can offload a significant share of its investment to the mega suppliers, and thus improve return on investments, and remunerate them once it receives payment from the customer. In addition, as mega suppliers deliver large integrated sections of the aircraft, the final assembly time is significantly reduced, which leads to reduced inventory costs.

Further, through readjusting their tiered structure and empowering mega suppliers, OEMs aim to decrease the cost of managing the value chain, as a comment of a former Boeing manager shows.

> *"We had tier-1 to 3: tier-1 are people [...] providing final assembly for us (e.g., wings, landing gears, engines)—completed components that were bolted together to assemble an airplane. For the 787 we wanted [...] to follow the tier structure to reduce our administrative cost. Tier-1 is systems, tier-2 is components, tier-3 is parts and pieces, tier-4, which was introduced later, is raw materials."*
> *(Former Executive Vice President at Boeing)*

With this approach, Boeing aims to reduce its total direct supplier base by 70% to less than 10,000 suppliers. Interview results indicate that overhead and labor costs are lower at lower levels of the tiered structure. Thus, the introduction of mega suppliers not only reduces complexity for the OEM but also the overall administrative and labor costs, thus increasing the value created.

Further, the ownership of a module by a mega supplier entails the assembly of the assigned section and the design and innovation to meet performance specifications provided by Boeing—a so-called build to performance approach. By outsourcing 60% of the design and production work of the 787, Boeing gave away a large share of its former activities. Boeing remains the high-level designer and integrator of the aircraft (assembling integrated subsystems supplied by partners) as well as the interface to the customers.

5.3 Conclusion

The case studies confirm the suggested determinants of bargaining structure—value chain and, in turn, product architecture as well as an individual firm's power. Thus, they can be used to shape bargaining structure, implement a hierarchy strategy, and increase value capture.

In both cases, value chain architecture mostly changed in parallel and coincided with bargaining structure. The BSH case illustrates how the strong link between product and value chain architecture can be used by firms to shape the bargaining structure already during the design phase of a product. Therefore, I argue that bargaining structure already needs to be considered in the design phase of the product to leverage its full potential. In contrast, the aircraft case shows that value chain architecture itself drives bargaining structure. Changes in value chain architecture do not necessarily lead to significant changes in the product architecture.

Further, the case studies confirm that powerful firms in the value chain, that is, firms that are hard to replace, have the ability to directly shape the bargaining structure. Realizing volume effects and the control over key components are presumably the main reasons for firms taking action and directly altering the bargaining structure. In particular, if there is a high commonality of components and input materials, these inputs are required in high volume across systems, and suppliers do not serve multiple customers, OEMs tend to directly negotiate prices for the supply omitting the intermediary tier-1 suppliers. However, both observations aim at building or strengthening a bottleneck position.

There is neither indication that bargaining structure per se was a reason for taking action nor that it is seen as a lever to increase value capture. Consequently, firms miss out on many opportunities to use bargaining structure to increase value capture. It remains to be discussed to what extent the hierarchy strategy stays in conflict to alternative strategies to increase value capture.

6 Discussion and conclusion

The analyses based on the game theoretic model in Chapter 4 indicate that the structure of negotiations along the value chain affects value distribution. Thus, besides considerations of replaceability, firms can aim to increase value capture by creating a beneficial bargaining structure. A bargaining structure is beneficial for a firm if it is positioned in those negotiations in which most complementarity gains are realized. In the commercial aircraft and laundry dryer industries, which are analyzed in the case studies, the OEMs' capabilities and assets, such as customer access, final integration, and project management capabilities, are critical, scarce resources. Consequently, the highest complementarities are realized on the top-level when the final product is assembled, making it highly beneficial for firms to be involved in top-level negotiations. However, these highest complementarity gains are not necessarily realized on the top-level of the bargaining structure. For example, some final modifications of existing products—such as underwater cameras that combine a camera and a waterproof case or modified trucks that are standard trucks with specialized truck-type mounting—negotiated on the top-level tend to have a low value add relative to the value of the core product. As most complementarity is realized in the negotiations on the core product, that is, on the second level of the bargaining structure, suppliers of additional features would benefit from being moved to a lower level of the bargaining structure.

As seen in the case studies on the commercial aircraft and laundry dryer value chains, bargaining structures can be directly shaped through the action of individual firms or indirectly through the underlying value chains. First, some firms might have the power to change the bargaining structure without influencing the underlying value chain. In the instances observed, firms that are hard to replace directly modified the bargaining structure to build or strengthen a bottleneck position (e.g., through bundling purchasing volume or controlling key components); however, they did not shape it to enhance value capture with regard to the hierarchy strategy. Second, the results suggest that value chain architecture is a key determinant of bargaining structure. Changes in the value chain architecture, such as the introduction of system suppliers, were mostly reflected in the structure of negotiations along the value chain.

Further, the laundry dryer case study illustrates that the modular product architecture often mirrors the architecture of the value chain, as already suggested by Baldwin and Clark (2000), Chesbrough and Teece (1996), and Colfer and Baldwin (2010). Consequently, firms designing the overall modular product architecture have the opportunity to shape the value chain architecture and bargaining structure, given certain boundary conditions (e.g., technical limitations, capabilities of suppliers), to implement a hierarchy strategy. Among other things, decisions on the number and composition of top-level modules determine the bargaining structure and value capture of the system designer. This implies a need to involve various organizational functions besides the technical department during the design of the product architecture, such as strategy and procurement, to identify and implement product architectures and value chain architectures that entail beneficial bargaining structures.

Further, the degree of hierarchy in a bargaining structure affects the value capture of firms with a portfolio of business activities that target different parts of the same value chain. As the aircraft case revealed, different positions of a firm often cannot be kept separate in a non-hierarchical bargaining structure, which can reduce value capture. In contrast, a hierarchical bargaining structure may allow a firm owning several bargaining positions in different parts of the structure to keep them separate, thus, potentially increasing value capture. For example, multiple bottleneck positions of a conglomerate in a given value chain translate into essential bargaining positions. If the bottleneck positions refer to contributions to different parts of the product, that is, the focal firm supplies to firms in different parts of the value chain, and the bargaining structure mostly coincides with value chain architecture, the firm can take advantage of its essential positions in separate negotiations and increase the potential value capture. Consequently, as the bargaining structure affects the value capture of any second position in the bargaining structure, it needs to be carefully considered in the context of mergers and acquisitions of firms within the same value chain.

Having seen that a given bargaining structure favors some firms, the question arises why firms that stand to lose from a particular bargaining structure would nonetheless accept it. I argue that firms only involved in lower-level negotiation often do not have full transparency of the overall bargaining structure, in particular in large value chains of complex products. Further, not all firms have the power to influence bargaining structures. Firms that are easily replaceable are not able to change the bargaining structure or the underlying value chain architecture in such a way to create disadvantages for more powerful firms. Nevertheless, to maintain a healthy and robust industry, there are limits to the execution of the hierarchy strategy. In particular, the value capture of every firm needs to match at least the outside options beyond the focal value chain.

There are several limitations of my analysis. First, it does not account for the fact that value chain architecture and bargaining structure may affect the overall value created. For example, splitting essential positions in excess to increase own value capture will hurt value creation not only because of increased transaction costs. Too many firms with essential positions having the ability to block value creation lead to an underuse of resources, a phenomenon known as the tragedy of the anticommons (Heller and Eisenberg 1998). It occurs, for example, in the context of patent royalty stacking (Lemley and Shapiro 2007; Shapiro 2001) in which multiple essential patent owners, each creating a holdup risk, may increase the overall price beyond the monopoly level (Cournot 1838) and lead to stifling innovation. Ziedonis (2004) provides evidence that patent royalty stacking is an issue in the semiconductor industry.

Similarly, the cost of changing and operating bargaining structures has not been considered in the model. In particular, in settings of existing buyer-supplier relationships the reorganization of the bargaining structure might cause additional costs and negatively affect the relations between firms. In addition, the transaction costs associated with different bargaining structures might differ. Thus, also for these reasons, a change in bargaining structures potentially affects the absolute value to be distributed.

Further, the present work does not discuss the interdependency between the hierarchy strategy and other strategies to enhance value capture, that is, to what extent the strategies are in line or conflicting. The case studies indicate that changes in the bargaining structure—which were not seen as a lever per se—are often connected to changes in the value chain architecture, which may have an effect on the replaceability of firms. For example, to carve out the effects of changes in the bargaining structure, I assumed that a shift of integration capabilities from OEM to tier-1 suppliers, which goes along with a more hierarchical bargaining structure, does not affect the replaceability of the firms. As integration can also be done by the OEM, one can argue that the integration activity is in competitive supply, thus, the change does not affect the supplier's replaceability. Nevertheless, the supplier may reach a higher level of essentiality over time due to the interorganizational relationship, as suggested by Dyer and Singh (1998). Interconnected assets such as the colocation of production facilities, lack of alternative providers that have the complementary capabilities that were developed over time, and indivisibility of jointly developed capabilities and resources puts the partners in a mutual dependency. Thus, the change in value chain architecture affects replaceability of the tier-1 supplier. In general, it is not clear whether the effect of the change in bargaining structure counterbalances an (negative) effect of a change in replaceability. There are many reasons for choosing a particular bargaining structure, value chain architecture, or product architecture, and the hierarchy strategy is only one among them. It remains open to further study as to what extent the hierarchy strategy is in line with or conflicts with other strategies to enhance value capture.

In addition, value distribution might differ from the HSV estimates. Although the Shapley value showed relatively good predictive accuracy in empirical tests, real-world bargaining situations may be found to be more "unfair," meaning they might favor certain players that can extract even more value. An empirical test of the HSV in this context, that is, for hierarchical bargaining structures with limited transparency, could serve to assess its predictive accuracy. Further, besides the distribution concept, the effect of bargaining structure on value capture needs to be analyzed in real-world settings. Situations in which only the bargaining structure changes while everything else remains more or less constant, in particular, the replaceability of firms, can be considered promising cases for analysis. As observed in the aircraft industry, potential settings might include cases in which OEMs that once negotiated with lower tier suppliers eliminated their intermediary position and readjusted the bargaining structure to the value chain architecture. If there are no concurrent changes in the value chain architecture and no significant changes in replaceability (e.g., through increasing purchasing volume), then replaceability remains constant and the effect of bargaining structure should become visible.

Possible extensions of the model could consider the emergence of the value chain, which determines the overall value generated and distributed. Taking the value as non-constant, which could potentially be modeled as a biform game as proposed by Brandenburger and Stuart (2007), might provide an interesting perspective on how the anticipation of eventual bargaining structures could matter during establishment of the value chain.

The present work contributes to the literature in several ways. First, the HSV concept complements the extensions of the Shapley value in the area of cooperative game theory. The concept mirrors negotiations in a tree-like hierarchical structure in the light of limited transparency of participants. In contrast to other concepts, players have information only on participants that are involved in the same negotiations and disregard negotiations in distant parts of the bargaining structure. Second, by showing how firms can enhance value appropriation through strategically shaping the structure of negotiations along the value chains, I add to the discussion of industry architectures as determinants of value appropriation. I refer to this approach as the hierarchy strategy, which complements the established bottleneck strategy. The study explains the determinants of bargaining structure, namely, value chain architecture and, in turn, product architecture, and the direct influence of powerful individuals. The findings can assist managers in identifying and shaping beneficial value chain and bargaining structures, thus, increasing value capture.

Appendices

Appendix A – Glossary

$M = \{m_j\}_{j=1,\dots,n}$	Set of $n \in \mathbb{N}$ bargaining firms (or bargaining positions if a firm participates more than once in the bargaining structure)
$C_e \subseteq M$	Set of essential firms in M such that $v(J) = 0$ if $C_e \nsubseteq J$
M_{int}	Set of system integrators
m_{NVA}	Non-value-appropriating firm that is not part of the bargaining structure
M_{NVA}	L1 cluster containing m_{NVA} in the hypothetical hierarchical bargaining structure in which m_{NVA} is value-appropriating
$\mathfrak{B} = \{M_i\}_{i=1,\dots,k}$	Hierarchical bargaining structure, that is, a partition of firms into $k \in \mathbb{N}$ clusters $M_1, \dots, M_k$
$\lvert . \rvert$	Cardinality or size of a set
$n!$	Factorial of a positive integer, that is, the product of all positive integers less or equal than n
$v: 2^M \to \mathbb{R}$	Characteristic function assigning every subset of firms $J \subseteq M$ a real value $v(J)$
$\hat{v}: 2^{\mathfrak{B}} \to \mathbb{R}$	Induced characteristic function based on v, assigning every subset of clusters $J \subseteq \mathfrak{B}$ a real value $\hat{v}(J) = v\left(\bigcup_{M_i \in J} M_i\right)$
$\breve{v}_{M_i}: 2^{M_i} \to \mathbb{R}$	Induced characteristic function based on v, assigning every subset of firms in a cluster of the hierarchical bargaining structure $J \subseteq M_i \in \mathfrak{B}$ a real value $\tilde{v}_{M_i}(J) = \frac{(v(J \cup (M \setminus M_i)) - v(M \setminus M_i))}{v(M) - v(M \setminus M_i)} \phi_{M_i}(\hat{v})$
$v^{int}: 2^{M \cup M_{int}} \to \mathbb{R}$	Induced characteristic function based on v, assigning every subset of firms in a bargaining structure with system integrators $J \subseteq M \cup M_{int}$ a real value $v^{int}(J)$ (see Equation (13), pg. 48)

$v'': 2^{M \cup m_{NVA}} \to \mathbb{R}$	Characteristic function assigning every subset of firms $J \subseteq M \cup m_{NVA}$ in the hypothetical case that m_{NVA} is value-appropriating a real value $v''(J)$
$\breve{v}''_{M_i}: 2^{M \cup m_{NVA}} \to \mathbb{R}$	Induced characteristic function based on v'', assigning every subset of firms $J \subseteq M \cup m_{NVA}$ (in the hypothetical case that m_{NVA} is value-appropriating) a real value $\breve{v}''_{M_i}(J)$, which is defined analog to $\breve{v}_{M_i}$
$v': 2^M \to \mathbb{R}$	Induced characteristic function based on v'', assigning every subset of firms $J \subseteq M$ a real value $v'(J) = v''(J \cup m_{NVA})$ (distributing the value add of m_{NVA})
$\hat{v}': 2^{\mathfrak{B}} \to \mathbb{R}$	Induced characteristic function based on v'', assigning every subset of clusters $J \subseteq \mathfrak{B}$ a real value $\hat{v}'(J)$ with $\hat{v}'(J) = v''\left(\bigcup_{M_i \in J} M_i \cup m_{NVA}\right)$ if $J \cap M_{NVA} \neq \emptyset$ and $\hat{v}'(J) = \hat{v}(J)$ if $J \cap M_{NVA} = \emptyset$
$\breve{v}'_{M_i}: 2^M \to \mathbb{R}$	Induced characteristic function based on $\breve{v}''_{M_i}$, assigning every subset of firms $J \subseteq M$ a real value $\breve{v}'_{M_i}(J) := \breve{v}''_{M_i}(J \cup m_{NVA})$ if $J \cap M_i \neq \emptyset$ and $\breve{v}'_{M_i}(J) := \breve{v}''_{M_i}(J)$ if $J \cap M_i = \emptyset$
$v_S^{M_i}: 2^{\mathfrak{B}} \to \mathbb{R}$	Induced characteristic function based on v and $S \subseteq M_i$, assigning every set of clusters of the hierarchical bargaining structure $J \subseteq \mathfrak{B}$ a real value $v_S^{M_i}(J)$, with $v_S^{M_i}(J) = v\left(\bigcup_{M_l \in J} M_l \setminus \bar{S}\right)$
$v^{M_i}: 2^{M_i} \to \mathbb{R}$	Induced characteristic function based on $v_S^{M_i}$, assigning every subset of firms $J \in M_i$ a real value $v^{M_i}(J) = \phi_{M_i}(v_J^{M_i})$
$v\|_{M_i}: 2^{M_i} \to \mathbb{R}$	Restricted characteristic function based on v and $M_i \in \mathfrak{B}$, assigning every subset of firms $J \subseteq M_i$ a real value $v\|_{M_i}(S) = v(S)$
$v^y_{M_i}: 2^{M_i} \to \mathbb{R}$	Induced characteristic function based on v and $y \in C(\mathfrak{B}, \hat{v})$, assigning every subset of firms $J \in M_i$ a real value $v^y_{M_i}(J) = \begin{cases} y_i & if\ J = M_i \\ \max\limits_{S \subseteq \mathfrak{B} \setminus M_i} \left\{ v\left(\bigcup_{M_j \in S} M_j \cup J\right) - y(S) \right\} & if\ J \subset M_i \end{cases}$

$v_{M_i}^{y\,*}: 2^{M_i} \to \mathbb{R}$	Induced characteristic function based on v and $y \in C(\mathfrak{B}, \hat{v})$, assigning every subset of firms $J \in M_i$ a real value $v_{M_i}^{y\,*}(J) := \begin{cases} y_i & if\ J = M_i \\ \max\{0; v(J \cup M \backslash M_i) - y(M \backslash M_i)\} & if\ J \subset M_i \end{cases}$
$\Delta_{J,K}$	Complementarity gains between two sets of firms $J, K \subseteq M$ and $J \cap K = \emptyset$, that is, $v(J \cup K) - v(J) - v(K)$
$\Delta_{J,K,L}$	Complementarity gains between two sets of firms $J, K, L \subseteq M$ and $J \cap K = \emptyset$, that is, $v(J \cup K \cup L) - v(J) - v(K) - v(L)$
$\phi_{m_j}(v)$	Value capture of firm m_j according to Shapley value based on the characteristic function v (see Equation (1), pg. 20)
$\phi_{M_i}(\hat{v}, \mathfrak{B})$	Value capture of a cluster of firms M_i in top-level negotiations in a hierarchical bargaining structure $\mathfrak{B}$ according to Shapley value, based on the induced characteristic function $\hat{v}$ (see Equation (3), pg. 22)
$\phi_{m_j}^{HSV}(v) = \phi_{m_j}^{HSV}(\check{v}_{M_i}, \mathfrak{B})$	Value capture of firm m_j in a hierarchical bargaining structure $\mathfrak{B}$ with $m_j \in M_i \in \mathfrak{B}$ according to the hierarchical Shapley value, based on the induced characteristic function $\tilde{v}_{M_i}$(see Equation (4), pg. 22)
$\phi_{m_j}^{OV}(v) = \phi_{m_j}^{OV}(v^{M_i})$	Value capture of firm m_j in a hierarchical bargaining structure $\mathfrak{B}$ with $m_j \in M_i \in \mathfrak{B}$ according to the Owen value, based on the induced characteristic function v^{M_i} (see Equation (17), pg. 60)
$\phi_{m_j}^{M_i}(v\|_{M_i})$	Value capture of firm m_j in a hierarchical bargaining structure $\mathfrak{B}$ with $m_j \in M_i \in \mathfrak{B}$ according to the $\mathfrak{B}$-value, based on the restricted characteristic function $v\|_{M_i}$ (see Equation (18), pg. 64)
$x \in \mathbb{R}^{\|M\|}$	The vector of value capture of all firms in M
$x: 2^M \to \mathbb{R}$	Sum of value capture of a set of firms $J \subseteq M$, that is, $x(J) = \sum_{i \in J} x_i$ with x_i being the i-th component of x

$C(M, v)$	Value distribution among firms in M according to the Core, based on the characteristic function v (see Equation (19) pg. 65)
$CC(M, v, \mathfrak{B})$	Value distribution among firms in a hierarchical bargaining structure according to the coalitional Core, based on the characteristic function v (see Equation (20), pg. 66)
$HC(M, v, \mathfrak{B})$	Value distribution among firms in a hierarchical bargaining structure according to the hierarchical Core, based on the characteristic function v (see Equation (22), pg. 67)
Δ_m^{HSV}	Difference of value capture of a firm $m \in M$ in a hierarchical and a non-hierarchical bargaining structure (according to the hierarchical Shapley value and Shapley value, respectively) relative to the overall value being distributed in M, that is $\frac{(\phi_m^{HSV}(v) - \phi_m(v))}{v(M)}$

Appendix B – Properties of the HSV

In the following, I check if the HSV fulfills the properties of efficiency, invariance under dummy players, additivity, symmetry across coalitions, and symmetry within coalitions.

Efficiency:

Let $i: \{1, \dots, n\} \rightarrow \{1, \dots k\}$ be the mapping that assigns every element $m_j \in M$ its cluster $M_{i(j)} \in \mathfrak{B}$. It holds that

$$\sum_{m_j \in M} \phi_{m_j}^{HSV}(v) = \sum_{m_j \in M} \phi_{m_j}^{HSV}\left(\check{v}_{M_{i(j)}}, \mathfrak{B}\right) = \sum_{M_i \in \mathfrak{B}} \sum_{m_j \in M_i} \phi_{m_j}^{HSV}\left(\check{v}_{M_i}, \mathfrak{B}\right)$$

$$= \sum_{M_i \in \mathfrak{B}} \phi_{M_i}(\hat{v}, \mathfrak{B}) = \hat{v}(\mathfrak{B}) = v(M)$$

Invariance under dummy players:

Let $m_j \in M$ be a dummy player, that is, $v(J \cup m_j) - v(J) = 0 \; \forall J \subset M$. Then,

$$\phi_{m_j}^{HSV}(v) = \sum_{S \subseteq M_i \setminus \{m_j\}} \frac{|S|! \, (|M_i| - |S| - 1)!}{|M_i|!} \left(\check{v}_{M_i}(S \cup \{m_j\}) - \check{v}_{M_i}(S)\right).$$

Further, as m_j is a dummy player in v and

$$\check{v}_{M_i}(S \cup \{m_j\}) - \check{v}_{M_i}(S)$$

$$= \frac{\left(v\left(S \cup \{m_j\} \cup (M \setminus M_i)\right) - v\left(S \cup (M \setminus M_i)\right)\right) \phi_{M_i}(\hat{v}, \mathfrak{B})}{v(M) - v(M \setminus M_i)} = 0,$$

it holds that $\phi_{m_j}^{HSV}(v) = 0$.

Additivity:

Let $v: 2^M \rightarrow \mathbb{R}$ and $w: 2^M \rightarrow \mathbb{R}$ be two games with $(v + w)(J) = v(J) + w(J)$. As $\left(\check{v}_{M_i} + \check{w}_{M_i}\right)(J) \neq \check{v}_{M_i}(J) + \check{w}_{M_i}(J)$ holds for $m_j \in M_i$ it follows that $\phi_{m_j}^{HSV}(v + w) \neq \phi_{m_j}^{HSV}(v) + \phi_{m_j}^{HSV}(w)$. Therefore, the HSV does not fulfill additivity.

Symmetry across coalitions:

Let $M_i, M_k \in \mathfrak{B}$ be symmetric in v, that is, $v(J \cup M_i) = v(J \cup M_k)$ for all $J \subset \mathfrak{B}$, $M_i \neq M_k$. It needs to be shown that $\sum_{m_j \in M_i} \phi_{m_j}^{HSV}(v) = \sum_{m_j \in M_k} \phi_{m_j}^{HSV}(v)$.

As the game the value distribution on L1 is defined by the Shapley value on the partition $\mathfrak{B}$, it follows from the symmetry of the Shapley value that $\phi_{M_i}(\hat{v}, \mathfrak{B}) = \phi_{M_k}(\hat{v}, \mathfrak{B})$. As $\sum_{m_j \in M_i} \phi_{m_j}^{HSV}(v) = \phi_{M_i}(\hat{v}, \mathfrak{B})$ and $\sum_{m_j \in M_k} \phi_{m_j}^{HSV}(v) = \phi_{M_k}(\hat{v}, \mathfrak{B})$, symmetry across coalitions follows directly.

Symmetry within coalitions:

Let $m_j, m_k \in M_i$ be symmetric in v, that is, $v(J \cup m_j) = v(J \cup m_k)$ for all $J \subset M$, $m_j \neq m_k$. It needs to be shown that $\phi_{m_j}^{HSV}(v) = \phi_{m_k}^{HSV}(v)$.

$$\phi_{m_j}^{HSV}(v) = \phi_{m_j}^{HSV}(\check{v}_{M_i}, \mathfrak{B})$$

$$= \sum_{S \subseteq M_i \setminus \{m_j\}} \frac{|S|!\,(|M_i| - |S| - 1)!}{|M_i|!} \left(\check{v}_{M_i}(S \cup \{m_j\}) - \check{v}_{M_i}(S)\right)$$

$$= \sum_{S' \subseteq M_i \setminus \{m_j, m_k\}} \frac{|S'|!\,(|M_i| - |S'| - 1)!}{|M_i|!} \left(\check{v}_{M_i}(S' \cup \{m_j\}) - \check{v}_{M_i}(S')\right)$$
$$+ \sum_{\substack{S'' \subseteq M_i \setminus \{m_j\}: \\ m_k \in S}} \frac{|S''|!\,(|M_i| - |S''| - 1)!}{|M_i|!} \left(\check{v}_{M_i}(S'' \cup \{m_j\}) - \check{v}_{M_i}(S'')\right)$$

The subsets of $M_i \setminus \{m_j\}$ are split into two groups; one group consisting of all subsets S' with $m_k \notin S'$, the other group consisting of all subsets S'' with $m_k \in S''$. Note that for every element S'' of the second group there exists a $S' \subseteq M_i \setminus \{m_j, m_k\}$ so that $S'' = S' \cup m_k$. It follows:

$$\phi_{m_j}^{HSV}(\check{v}_{M_i}, \mathfrak{B}) = \sum_{S' \subseteq M_i \setminus \{m_j, m_k\}} \frac{|S'|!\,(|M_i| - |S'| - 1)!}{|M_i|!} \left(\check{v}_{M_i}(S' \cup \{m_j\}) - \check{v}_{M_i}(S')\right)$$
$$+ \frac{(|S'| + 1)!\,(|M_i| - |S'|)!}{|M_i|!} \left(\check{v}_{M_i}(S' \cup \{m_k\} \cup \{m_j\}) - \check{v}_{M_i}(S' \cup \{m_k\})\right)$$

$$= \sum_{S' \subseteq M_i \backslash \{m_j, m_k\}} \frac{|S'|!\,(|M_i| - |S'| - 1)!}{|M_i|!} \left(\check{v}_{M_i}(S' \cup \{m_k\}) - \check{v}_{M_i}(S')\right)$$

$$+ \frac{(|S'| + 1)!\,(|M_i| - |S'|)!}{|M_i|!} \left(\check{v}_{M_i}\left(S' \cup \{m_k\} \cup \{m_j\}\right) - \check{v}_{M_i}\left(S' \cup \{m_j\}\right)\right)$$

$$= \sum_{J \subseteq M_i \backslash \{m_k\}} \frac{|J|!\,(|M_i| - |J| - 1)!}{|M_i|!} \left(\check{v}_{M_i}(J \cup \{m_k\}) - \check{v}_{M_i}(J)\right) = \phi_{m_k}^{HSV}\left(\check{v}_{M_i}, \mathfrak{B}\right)$$

Taking advantage of the fact that for every $S'' \subseteq M_i \backslash \{m_j\}: m_k \in S''$ a subset $J'' \subseteq M_i \backslash \{m_k\}: m_j \in J''$ with $J'' = S'' \backslash \{m_k\} \cup \{m_j\}$ and $|J''| = |S''|$ can be defined.

Appendix C – Forming the first cluster in bargaining structures with non-essential symmetric firms

Let M be a bargaining structure consisting of $n \in \mathbb{N}$ firms. Let $v: 2^M \to \mathbb{R}$ be the characteristic function with $v(J) = \alpha_j$ for all $J \subseteq M$ with $|J| = j$ and $0 = \alpha_0 \leq \alpha_1 \leq \cdots \leq \alpha_n = 1$.

In the following, I show that if there are no essential firms and all firms participate directly in top-level negotiations, that is, there are no clusters, it would be beneficial for a firm to form a two-firm cluster if $\alpha_{n-1} - \alpha_n > \frac{n-2}{n}$.

As all firms are symmetric, the value capture in the non-hierarchical case is $\phi_{m_j} = \frac{1}{n}$ for all $m_j \in M$. Without loss of generality, let $\{m_1, m_2\} =: m_1m_2$ be a cluster. Hence, $\mathfrak{B} = M \backslash \{m_1, m_2\} \cup \{m_1m_2\}$. It follows that

$$\phi_{m_1m_2}(\hat{v}, \mathfrak{B}) = \sum_{S \subseteq \mathfrak{B} \backslash \{m_1m_2\}} \frac{|S|!\,(n - |S| - 2)!}{(n-1)!} \big(\hat{v}(S \cup \{m_1m_2\}) - \hat{v}(S)\big)$$

$$= \sum_{j=0}^{n-2} \frac{(n-2)!}{(n-2-j)!\,j!} * \frac{j!\,(n-j-2)!}{(n-1)!} (\alpha_{j+2} - \alpha_j)$$

$$= \sum_{j=0}^{n-2} \frac{1}{n-1} (\alpha_{j+2} - \alpha_j)$$

$$= \frac{1}{n-1} (\alpha_n + \alpha_{n-1} - \alpha_1) = \frac{1}{n-1} (1 + \alpha_{n-1} - \alpha_1).$$

Further, it holds that

$$\phi_{m_1}^{HSV}(v) = \frac{\phi_{m_1m_2}(\hat{v}, \mathfrak{B})}{2(1 - \alpha_{n-2})} \big(v(M \backslash \{m_2\}) - v(M \backslash \{m_1m_2\}) + v(M) - v(M \backslash \{m_1\})\big)$$

$$= \frac{1}{2} \phi_{m_1m_2}(\hat{v}, \mathfrak{B}).$$

Consequently, forming a two-firm cluster is beneficial for m_1 (and m_2) if

$$\frac{1}{2(n-1)} (1 + \alpha_{n-1} - \alpha_1) > \frac{1}{n} \Leftrightarrow \alpha_{n-1} - \alpha_1 > \frac{n-2}{2}$$

Appendix D – Analysis of three-firm bargaining structure relaxing the assumption of symmetry

In the following, three-firm bargaining structures without the assumption of symmetry among non-essential firms are analyzed. The analysis is limited to the case of two non-essential firms because the symmetry assumption does not affect the cases with less than two non-essential firms, and the case of three non-essential firms has already been discussed in the beginning of Section 4.2.1.

The bargaining structure consists again of the firms $\{m_1, m_2, m_3\}$ that are clustered into two clusters $\{\{m_1 m_2\}, m_3\}$ in the hierarchical case. I distinguish among the non-essential firms so that each firm has a different value add to every group of firms. Hence, let $N_i, i \in \{1,2\}$ denote the non-essential firms and E denote the essential firm. Further, let $0 < \alpha \leq \beta_i \leq 1$ for $i \in \{1,2\}$. Let $v: 2^M \to \mathbb{R}$ be the characteristic function defined in the following way: $v(E) = \alpha$, $v(EN_i) = \beta_i$ for , $i \in \{1,2\}$, and $v(EN_1N_2) = 1$, and $v(J) = 0$ in all other cases.

Consequently, the SV distribution in the non-hierarchical case is $\phi_E = \frac{1}{3}(1 + \alpha + \frac{1}{2}(\beta_1 + \beta_2))$, $\phi_{N_1} = \frac{1}{6}(2 - \alpha + \beta_1 - 2\beta_2)$, $\phi_{N_2} = \frac{1}{6}(2 - \alpha + \beta_2 - 2\beta_1)$. The HSV distribution can be found in Table 22.

Based on the analysis in Table 23, the following result can be derived: If there is exactly one essential firm not being clustered with any non-essential firm in the bargaining structure (case 0-1), the essential firm can benefit from a hierarchical

# ess. firms in		L1-HSV of...		L2-HSV of firmss in $m_1 m_2$	
$m_1 m_2$	m_3	$m_1 m_2$	m_3	Essential	Non-essential
1	0	$\frac{1}{2}(1+\beta_1)$	$\frac{1}{2}(1-\beta_1)$	$\frac{(1+\beta_1)}{4}(1+\beta_2)$	$\frac{(1+\beta_1)}{4}(1-\beta_2)$
0	1	$\frac{1}{2}(1-\alpha)$	$\frac{1}{2}(1+\alpha)$	-	$N_1: \frac{1}{4}(1-\alpha+\beta_1-\beta_2)$ $N_2: \frac{1}{4}(1-\alpha+\beta_2-\beta_1)$

Table 22: HSV for firms in three-firm bargaining structure without the assumption of symmetry

# of essential firms in m_1m_2 m_3		Who gains and who loses through a hierarchical bargaining structure
1	0	The **essential firm in m_1m_2** gains if and only if $\frac{1}{4}(1+\beta_1)(1+\beta_2) > \frac{1}{3}(1+\alpha+\frac{1}{2}(\beta_1+\beta_2))$ The **non-essential firm (N_1) in m_1m_2** gains if and only if $\frac{1}{4}(1+\beta_1)(1-\beta_2) > \frac{1}{6}(2-\alpha+\beta_1-2\beta_2)$ The **non-essential firm m_3 (N_2)** gains if and only if $\frac{1}{2}(1-\beta_1) > \frac{1}{6}(2-\alpha+\beta_2-2\beta_1) \Leftrightarrow 1-\beta_1 > \beta_2-\alpha \Leftrightarrow 1-\beta_2 > \beta_1-\alpha$, this is if and only if the complementarity is larger on top-level (from two to three firms) than within the cluster (for every two firms).
0	1	The **non-essential firm N_1 in m_1m_2** gains if and only if $\frac{1}{4}(1-\beta_2+\beta_1-\alpha) > \frac{1}{6}(2-\alpha+\beta_1-2\beta_2) \Leftrightarrow 1-\beta_1 < \beta_2-\alpha \Leftrightarrow 1-\beta_2 < \beta_1-\alpha$, this is if and only if complementarity is larger in the first step (for every two firms) than in the second step (from two to three firms).

Table 23: Analysis of three-firm bargaining structures without symmetry: For which firms is a hierarchical bargaining structure beneficial (compared to a non-hierarchical one)?

bargaining structure if the complementarity is higher in top-level negotiations than within the cluster, that is, the value add of a third firm joining is larger than the value add of any second firm joining the essential firm.

Appendix E – *n*-firm bargaining structures analyzed with the Owen value

Δ_m^{OV} for essential firm *E*	# of L1 clusters of firms: Minimum (2)	# of L1 clusters of firms: Maximum
E **not clustered with any non-essential firm** on L1	(A) 	(B) 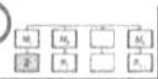
E clustered with **1 non-essential firm** on L1	(C) 	(D) 
E clustered with ***n*-2 non-essential firms** on L1	(E) 	

(A) Minimum (2), *E* not clustered with any non-essential firm on L1

Level of complementarity (x)	Number of firms (n): 3	10	100	10^6
1.5	1.7	6.5	9.5	10.0
2.0	3.7	12.0	16.2	16.7
2.5	5.7	16.4	20.9	21.4
3.0	7.4	19.8	24.5	25.0
20	16.7	38.7	44.7	45.2

(B) Maximum, *E* not clustered with any non-essential firm on L1

Level of complementarity (x)	Number of firms (n): 3	10	100	10^6
1.5	0	0	0	0
2.0	0	0	0	0
2.5	0	0	0	0
3.0	0	0	0	0
20	0	0	0	0

(C) Minimum (2), *E* clustered with 1 non-essential firm on L1

Level of complementarity (x)	Number of firms (n): 3	10	100	10^6
1.5	-0.9	4.3	9.2	10.0
2.0	-1.9	8.0	15.7	16.7
2.5	-2.8	11.0	20.3	21.4
3.0	-3.7	13.2	23.8	25.0
20	-8,3	16.7	40.2	45.2

(D) Maximum, *E* clustered with 1 non-essential firm on L1

Level of complementarity (x)	Number of firms (n): 3	10	100	10^6
1.5	-0.9	-0.7	-0.1	>-0.1
2.0	-1.9	-1.3	-0.2	>-0.1
2.5	-2.9	-1.8	-0.2	>-0.1
3.0	-3.7	-2.2	-0.2	>-0.1
20	-8.3	-4.3	-0.5	>-0.1

(E) *E* clustered with *n*-2 non-essential firms on L1

Level of complementarity (x)	Number of firms (n): 3	10	100	10^6
1.5	-0.9	-0.7	-0.1	>-0.1
2.0	-1.9	-1.3	-0.2	>-0.1
2.5	-2.9	-1.8	-0.2	>-0.1
3.0	-3.7	-2.2	-0.2	>-0.1
20	-8.3	-4.3	-0.5	>-0.1

Table 24: Relative difference (Δ_m^{OV}) between value appropriation in hierarchical and non-hierarchical bargaining structures for essential firm *E*

Δ_m^{OV} for non–essential firm clustered with *E* (on L1)	# of L1 clusters of firms: Minimum (2)	# of L1 clusters of firms: Maximum
***E* not clustered with any non-essential firm** on L1	(A) 	(B) 
E clustered with **1 non-essential firm** on L1	(C) 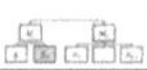	(D) 
E clustered with ***n*-2 non-essential firms** on L1	(E) 	

(A) Minimum (2), *E* not clustered with any non-essential firm on L1

Level of complementarity (x)	Number of firms (n): 3	10	100	10^6
1.5				
2.0				
2.5		n/a		
3.0				
20				

(B) Maximum, *E* not clustered with any non-essential firm on L1

Level of complementarity (x)	Number of firms (n): 3	10	100	10^6
1.5				
2.0				
2.5		n/a		
3.0				
20				

(C) Minimum (2), *E* clustered with 1 non-essential firm on L1

Level of complementarity (x)	Number of firms (n): 3	10	100	10^6
1.5	-0.9	-1.0	-0.2	>-0.1
2.0	-1.9	-1.3	-0.2	>-0.1
2.5	-2.8	-1.2	-0.1	>-0.1
3.0	-3.7	-0.8	>-0.1	>-0.1
20	-8.3	12.1	3.6	<0.1

(D) Maximum, *E* clustered with 1 non-essential firm on L1

Level of complementarity (x)	Number of firms (n): 3	10	100	10^6
1.5	-0.9	-0.7	-0.1	>-0.1
2.0	-1.9	-1.3	-0.2	>-0.1
2.5	-2.9	-1.8	-0.2	>-0.1
3.0	-3.7	-2.2	-0.2	>-0.1
20	-8.3	-4.3	-0.5	>-0.1

(E) *E* clustered with *n*-2 non-essential firms on L1

Level of complementarity (x)	Number of firms (n): 3	10	100	10^6
1.5	-0.9	-0.1	>-0.1	>-0.1
2.0	-1.9	-0.2	>-0.1	>-0.1
2.5	-2.8	-0.3	>-0.1	>-0.1
3.0	-3.7	-0.5	>-0.1	>-0.1
20	-8.3	-3.7	-0.1	>-0.1

Table 25: Relative difference (Δ_m^{OV}) between value appropriation in hierarchical and non-hierarchical bargaining structures for a non-essential firm being part of the same cluster as *E*

Δ_m^{OV} for non−essential firm not clustered with E (on L1)	# of L1 clusters of firms: Minimum (2)	# of L1 clusters of firms: Maximum
E **not clustered with any non-essential firm** on L1	A	B
E clustered with **1 non-essential firm** on L1	C	D
E clustered with ***n-2*** **non-essential firms** on L1	E	

A (Minimum (2); E not clustered with any non-essential firm on L1)

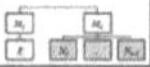

Level of complementarity (x)	Number of firms (n): *3*	*10*	*100*	*10⁶*
1.5	-0.9	-0.7	-0.1	>-0.1
2.0	-1.9	-1.3	-0.2	>-0.1
2.5	-2.8	-1.8	-0.2	>-0.1
3.0	-3.7	-2.2	-0.2	>-0.1
20	-8.3	-4.3	-0.5	>-0.1

B (Maximum; E not clustered with any non-essential firm on L1)

Level of complementarity (x)	Number of firms (n): *3*	*10*	*100*	*10⁶*
1.5	0	0	0	0
2.0	0	0	0	0
2.5	0	0	0	0
3.0	0	0	0	0
20	0	0	0	0

C (Minimum (2); E clustered with 1 non-essential firm on L1)

Level of complementarity (x)	Number of firms (n): *3*	*10*	*100*	*10⁶*
1.5	1.7	-0.4	-0.1	>-0.1
2.0	3.7	-0.8	-0.2	>-0.1
2.5	5.6	-1.2	-0.2	>-0.1
3.0	7.4	-1.5	-0.2	>-0.1
20	16.7	-3,6	-0.4	>-0.1

D (Maximum; E clustered with 1 non-essential firm on L1)

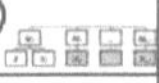

Level of complementarity (x)	Number of firms (n): *3*	*10*	*100*	*10⁶*
1.5	1.7	0.2	<0.1	<0.1
2.0	3.7	0.3	<0.1	<0.1
2.5	5.7	0.5	<0.1	<0.1
3.0	7.4	0.6	<0.1	<0.1
20	16.7	1.1	<0.1	<0.1

E (E clustered with *n-2* non-essential firms on L1)

Level of complementarity (x)	Number of firms (n): *3*	*10*	*100*	*10⁶*
1.5	1.7	1.2	0.1	<0.1
2.0	3.7	2.7	0.3	<0.1
2.5	5.6	4.2	0.5	<0.1
3.0	7.4	5.8	0.7	<0.1
20	16.7	34.1	8.1	<0.1

Table 26: Relative difference (Δ_m^{OV}) between value appropriation in hierarchical and non-hierarchical bargaining structures for a non-essential firm not being part of the same cluster as E

Appendix F – Hierarchical Core

In the following, it is shown that

$$HC(M, v, \mathfrak{B}) = \{x \in \mathbb{R}^{|M|} | x(M) = v(M), x(J) \geq v(J) \forall J \in \Omega_{\mathfrak{B}}^*\}$$

with $\Omega_{\mathfrak{B}}^* = \{R \subseteq M | R = K \cup M/M_i \; with \; K \subseteq M_i, M_i \in \mathfrak{B}\}$. The approach is similar to the proof for the Coalitional Core in Pulido and Sánchez-Sorino (2009).

On the one side, let $x \in HC(M, v, \mathfrak{B})$. Through the construction of the HC it follows that $x_{\mathfrak{B}} = (x(M_1), \dots, x(M_k)) \in C(\mathfrak{B}, \hat{v})$ and $x^{M_i} \in C(M_i, v_{M_i}^{x_{\mathfrak{B}}*})$ for all $M_i \in \mathfrak{B}$. It follows that

$$x(M) = \sum_{i=1:k} x(M_i) = \hat{v}(\mathfrak{B}) = v(M).$$

Let $R \in \Omega_{\mathfrak{B}}^*$. If $R = M \backslash M_i$ for some $M_i \in \mathfrak{B}$, then $x(R) \geq v(R)$ results from $x_{\mathfrak{B}} \in C(\mathfrak{B}, \hat{v})$. Let $R = J \cup M \backslash M_i$ with $J \subseteq M_i$ for some $M_i \in \mathfrak{B}$. From $x^{M_i} \in C(M_i, v_{M_i}^{x_{\mathfrak{B}}*})$ it follows that

$$\begin{aligned} x(R) = x(J) + \sum_{M_j \in \mathfrak{B} \backslash \{M_i\}} x(M_j) &\geq v_{M_i}^{x_{\mathfrak{B}}*}(J) + x_{\mathfrak{B}}(M \backslash M_i) \\ &= max\{0, v(J \cup M \backslash M_i) - x_{\mathfrak{B}}(M \backslash M_i)\} + x_{\mathfrak{B}}(M \backslash M_i) \\ &\geq v(J \cup M \backslash M_i) = v(R). \end{aligned}$$

Thus, if follows that $HC(M, v, \mathfrak{B}) \subseteq \{x \in \mathbb{R}^{|M|} | x(M) = v(M), x(J) \geq v(J) \forall J \in \Omega_{\mathfrak{B}}^*\}$.

On the other side, let $x \in \mathbb{R}^{|M|}$ such that $x(M) = v(M), x(J) \geq v(J) \forall J \in \Omega_{\mathfrak{B}}^*$. Let $x_{\mathfrak{B}} \in \mathbb{R}^{|\mathfrak{B}|}$ with $(x_{\mathfrak{B}})_i = x(M_i) \; \forall M_i \in \mathfrak{B}$ be defined as the quotient vector. As the coalitions of a priori unions are in $\Omega_{\mathfrak{B}}^*$ it follows that $x_{\mathfrak{B}} \in C(\mathfrak{B}, \hat{v})$.

It remains to be shown that $x^{M_i} \in C(M_i, v_{M_i}^{x_{\mathfrak{B}}*})$ for all $M_i \in \mathfrak{B}$. Let $M_i \in \mathfrak{B}, J \subset M_i$, then $J \cup M \backslash M_i \in \Omega_{\mathfrak{B}}^*$. It follows that $x(J \cup M \backslash M_i) \geq v(J \cup M \backslash M_i)$ and $x(J) \geq v(J \cup M \backslash M_i) - x_{\mathfrak{B}}(M \backslash M_i)$. Thus, it follows that $x(J) \geq v_{M_i}^{x_{\mathfrak{B}}*}(J)$. Further, by definition of the quotient vector it follows that $x^{M_i} \in C(M_i, v_{M_i}^{x_{\mathfrak{B}}*})$.

Appendix G – Questionnaire for case interviews

Guiding questions for BSH case interviews:

1) What was your position during the development and production of the T20 laundry dryer?

2) What was the role of your company for the T20? OEM, subsystem supplier, or tier-2 supplier?

3) What tasks did your company fulfill during the development and production of the T20?

4) Can you please name all components of the part that you produced?

5) To whom did you deliver your final parts? Which firms did supply you?

6) Which components and tasks did you contribute to the preceding product, the T10? How did your role and tasks change with the introduction of the T20?

7) To what extend did your responsibilities change?

8) [Only for subsystem suppliers] Are there any suppliers for whom you were responsible during the time of the T20, but who had been under the responsibility of (and directly supplied to) BSH beforehand (for the T10)? Which parts did they contribute?

9) [For OEM] Are there any tier-2 suppliers for whom you had been responsible beforehand (for the T10), but who supplied subsystem suppliers in course of the T20? Which parts did they contribute?

10) [For tier-2 suppliers] Did you supply (deliver to) another firm in the course of the T20 compared to the preceding product, the T10?

11) [For OEM and subsystem suppliers] To what extent was the management of tier-2 suppliers your responsibility? To what extent was the subsystem supplier [OEM respectively] involved?

12) Who was responsible for negotiations with tier-2 suppliers? To what extent was the OEM involved?

13) Who was responsible for negotiating prices with tier-2 suppliers? To what extent were OEM and subsystem supplier involved?

14) Were there any firms in the value chain that have a strong position, that is, they were hard to replace? Which firms?

15) How would assess your company's position in the T20 value chain? Would you have you been difficult to replace? How hard to replace were you?

16) Did your level of replaceability change with the introduction of the T20?

17) [If the area of responsibility increased] Which additional capabilities did you need to acquire for your new role in the T20 project? Did it affect your replaceability?

18) To what extent were you able to shape the modular product architecture of the T20 and the architecture of (and your position in) the value chain?

19) To what extend were you able to shape the bargaining structure, that is, the structure of price negotiations—who negotiates with whom?

20) What was the role of the OEM in this context?

21) From your point of view, what were the key factors that drove the bargaining structure and the architecture of the value chain?

22) [If there are differences between bargaining structure and value chain architecture] What were the reasons for the cases in which bargaining structure and value chain architecture did not match?

Appendix H – Brief profiles of interviewees

The following information is based on the case interviews and completed with information from the websites of the respective companies.

Interview 1: Harald Jungerberg, BSH Bosch und Siemens Hausgeräte GmbH
Case: Laundry dryer
Case related position: Project Director T20 at BSH Bosch und Siemens Hausgeräte GmbH
Date: 03/07/2014; *Duration*: 70 min
Method: Telephone interview with electronic recording

Interview 2: *Confidential*, BSH Bosch und Siemens Hausgeräte GmbH
Case: Laundry dryer
Case related position: Vice President Purchasing at BSH Bosch und Siemens Hausgeräte GmbH
Date: 09/07/2014; *Duration*: 62 min
Method: Telephone interview with electronic recording

Interview 3: Harald Jungerberg, BSH Bosch und Siemens Hausgeräte GmbH
Case: Laundry dryer
Case related position: Project Director T20 at BSH Bosch und Siemens Hausgeräte GmbH
Date: 16/07/2014; *Duration*: 31 min
Method: Telephone interview with electronic recording

Interview 4: Andreas Lange, Gerdes Kunststoff-Technik GmbH & Co. KG
Case: Laundry dryer
Case related position: Former responsible sales and project manager T20 at Coko-Werk GmbH & Co. KG
Date: 18/07/2014; *Duration*: 29 min
Method: Telephone interview with electronic recording

Interview 5: Dr. Michael Seikel, PAS Deutschland GmbH
Case: Laundry dryer
Case related position: Director Research and Development at Prettl (today, PAS Deutschland GmbH)

Date: 25/07/2014; *Duration*:47 min

Method: Telephone interview with electronic recording

Interview 6: Jano von Zitzewitz, Augsburg Innovationspark GmbH

Case: Commercial aircraft

Case related position: Former head of strategic procurement for metal components at Airbus

Date: 01/08/2014; *Duration*: 51 min

Method: Telephone interview with electronic recording

Interview 7: Ulf Sauerwald, Wirthwein Nauen GmbH & Co. KG

Case: Laundry dryer

Case related position: Factory manager at Wirthwein Nauen GmbH & Co. KG

Date: 02/09/2014; *Duration*: 27 min

Method: Telephone interview with electronic recording

Interview 8: *Confidential*

Case: Commercial aircraft

Case related position: Former Executive Vice President at Boeing

Date: 02/10/2014; *Duration*: 66 min

Method: Telephone interview with electronic recording

Interview 9: Ron Johnson, RJ Enterprises

Case: Commercial aircraft

Case related position: Former Vice President Engineering at Boeing [1996-2007]

Date: 02/10/2014; *Duration*: 35 min

Method: Telephone interview with electronic recording

Interview 10: Scott Andrew, SA Aerospace Consultancy Ltd.

Case: Commercial aircraft

Case related position: Former Senior Vice President Procurement Strategy at Airbus [2005-2010]

Date: 06/10/2014; *Duration*: 39 min

Method: Telephone interview with electronic recording

Interview 11: Edward Carson, Growth Management & Constructive Changes LLC

Case: Commercial aircraft

Case related position: Former Executive Vice President, HITCO Carbon Composites [2004-2009], former Senior Contract Manager and Senior Business Manager at Boeing [1972-2004]

Date: 13/10/2014; *Duration*: 53 min

Method: Telephone interview with electronic recording

Bibliography

Abernathy WJ, Utterback JM (1978) Patterns of industrial innovation. *Technology Review* 80(7):40-47.

Adegbesan JA (2009) On the origins of competitive advantage: Strategic factor markets and heterogeneous resource complementarity. *Academy of Management Review* 34(3):463-475.

Adner R, Zemsky P (2006) A demand-based perspective on sustainable competitive advantage. *Strategic Management Journal* 27(3):215-239.

Airbus (2014) *Airbus Approved Suppliers List*, May. Last accessed 23 Jun 2014, http://www.airbus.com/fileadmin/media_gallery/files/supply___world/Airbus-SupplierApprovalList-May-2014.pdf.

Airframer (2014). Last accessed 27 March 2014, http://www.airframer.com/.

Alchian AA, Demsetz H (1972) Production, information costs, and economic organization. *American Economic Review* 62(5):777-895.

Anton JJ, Yao DA (1995) Standard-setting consortia, antitrust, and high-technology industries. *Antitrust Law Journal* 64(1):247-265.

Aumann RJ, Drèze J (1974) Cooperative games with coalition structures. *International Journal of Game Theory* 3(4):217-237.

Aumann RJ, Shapley LS (1994) Long-term competition: A game-theoretic analysis. Megiddo N, eds. *Essays in Game Theory in Honor of Michael Maschler* (Springer, New York).

Bain J (1956) *Barriers to New Competition: Their Character and Consequences in Manufacturing Industries* (Harvard University Press, Cambridge, MA).

Baldwin CY (2014) Bottlenecks, Modules and Dynamic Architectural Capabilities. *Harvard Business School Finance Working Paper No. 15-028*, http://dash.harvard.edu/bitstream/handle/1/13350434/15-028.pdf?sequence=1.

Baldwin CY, Clark KB (1997) Managing in an age of modularity. *Harvard Business Review* 75(5):84-93.

Baldwin CY, Clark KB (2000) *Design Rules: The Power of Modularity*, Vol.1 (MIT Press, Cambridge, MA).

Baldwin CY, Clark KB (2000) *Design rules: The power of modularity*, Vol.1 (MIT Press, Cambridge).

Barney JB (1986) Strategic factor markets: Expectations, luck, and business strategy. *Management Science* 32(10):1231-1241.

Barney JB (1991) Firm resources and sustained competitive advantage. *Journal of Management* 17(1):99-120.

Bennett VM (2013) Organization and bargaining: Sales process choice at auto dealerships. *Management Science* 59(9):2003-2018.

Boeing (2009) *Boeing Quality Management System Requirements for Suppliers*. Last accessed 23 Jun 2014, http://www.boeingsuppliers.com/supplier/.

Bonacich P (1979) A single measure for point and interval predictions of coalition theories. *Behavioral Science* 24:85-93.

Bosch Siemens Hausgeräte GmbH (2014) *Gestaltung und Umsetzung der WäschetrocknerplattformT20* (Company presentation, Munich, 14 Oct 2014).

Bosch Siemens Hausgeräte GmbH (2014) *The Company - Figures & Facts*. Last accessed 28 Nov 2014, http://bsh-group.com/index.php?109439.

Bowman C, Ambrosini V (2000) Value creation versus value capture: Towards a coherent definition of value in strategy. *British Journal of Management* 11(1):1-15.

Brandenburger A, Stuart H (1996) Value-based business strategy. *Journal of Economics & Management Strategy* 5(1):5-24.

Brandenburger A, Stuart H (2007) Biform games. *Management Science* 53(4):537-549.

Buvik A, Reve T (2002) Inter-firm governance and structural power in industrial relationships: The moderating effect of bargaining power on the contractual safeguarding of specific assets. *Scandinavian Journal of Management* 18(3):261-284.

Cachon GP, Netessine S (2004) Game theory in supply chain analysis. Simchi-Levi D, Wu SD, Shen Z-J, eds. *Handbook of Quantitative Supply Chain Analysis: Modeling in the e-Business Era* (Springer, New York, NY).

Calmfors L, Driffill J, Honkapohja S, Giavazzi F (1988) Bargaining structure, corporatism and macroeconomic performance. *Economic policy* 3(6):14-61.

Camerer C (1991) Does strategy research need game theory? *Strategic Managemenf Journal* 12(S2):137-152.

Campbell DT (1975) Degrees of freedom and the case study. *Comparative Political Studies* 8:178-193.

Campbell DT, Stanley J (1963) *Experimental and Quasi Experimental Designs for Research* (Houghton Mifflin, Boston, MA).

Cassiolato JE, Bernardes R, Lastres H (2002) *Transfer of Technology for Successful Integration into the Global Economy: A Case Study of Embraer in Brazil* (UN, UNCTAD/UNDP Global Programme on Globalization, Liberalization and Sustainable Human Development, New York, NY).

Chatain O, Zemsky P (2007) The horizontal scope of the firm: Organizational tradeoffs vs. buyer-supplier relationships. *Management Science* 53(4):550-565.

Chesbrough HW (2003) *Open Innovation: The New Imperative for Creating and Profiting from Technology* (Harvard Business School Press, Boston, MA).

Chesbrough HW, Teece DJ (1996) When is virtual virtuous? Organizing for innovation. *Harvard Business Review* 74(1):65-74.

Clark KB (1985) The interaction of design hierarchies and market concepts in technological evolution. *Research Policy* 14(5):235-251.

Colfer L, Baldwin CY (2010) The mirroring hypothesis: Theory, evidence and exceptions. *Harvard Business School Finance Working Paper No. 10-058*, http://papers.ssrn.com/sol3/papers.cfm?abstract_id=1539592.

Corbin J, Strauss A (2008) *Basics of Qualitative Research: Techniques and Procedures for Developing Grounded Theory* (SAGE Publications, Thousand Oaks, CA).

Cournot A (1838) *Researches into the Mathematical Principles of the Theory of Wealth* (MacMillan Company, New York, NY).

Daft R (1983) *Organization Theory and Design* (West, New York, NY).

Dedrick J, Kraemer KL, Linden G (2010) Who profits from innovation in global value chains: A study of the iPod and notebook PCs. *Industrial and Corporate Change* 19(1):81-116.

Dyer JH, Singh H (1998) The relational view: Cooperative strategy and sources of interorganizational competitive advantage. *Academy of Management Review* 23(4):660-679.

Edmondson AC, McManus SE (2007) Methodological fit in management field research. *Academy of Management Review* 32(4):1246-1264.

Eisenhardt KM (1989) Building theories from case study research. *Academy of Management Review* 14(4):532-550.

Eisenhardt KM, Graebner ME (2007) Theory building from cases: Opportunities and challenges. *Academy of Management Journal* 50(1):25-32.

Eisenmann TR, Parker G, Van Alstyne M (2009) Opening Platforms: How, When and Why? Gawer A, eds. *Platforms, markets and innovation* (Edward Elgar Publishing, Cheltenham, UK).

Elahi E, Sheikhzadeh M, Lamba N (2014) An integrated outsourcing framework: Analyzing Boeing's outsourcing program for Dreamliner (B787). *Knowledge and Process Management* 21(1):13-28.

Erat S, Kavadias S, Gaimon C (2013) The pitfalls of subsystem integration: When less is more. *Management Science* 59(3):659-676.

Feldhusen J, Grote K-H, Göpfert J., Tretow G (2013) Technische Systeme. Pahl G, Beitz W., Feldhusen J, Grote K-H *Pahl/Beitz Konstruktionslehre: Methoden und Anwendung erfolgreicher Produktentwicklung*, Vol.8 (Springer-Verlag, Berlin, Germany).

Ferraro F, Gurses K (2009) Building architectural advantage in the US motion picture industry: Lew Wasserman and the Music Corporation of America. *European Management Review* 6(4):233-249.

Gan T, Grunow M (2013) Concurrent product-supply chain design: A conceptual framework & literature review. *Procedia CIRP* 7:91-96.

Gawer A, Cusumano MA (2002) *Platform leadership* (Harvard Business School Press, Boston).

Gibbert M, Ruigrok W, Wicki B (2008) What passes as a rigorous case study? *Strategic Management Journal* 29(13):1465-1474.

Gillies DB (1953) Some Theorems on n-Person Games. *Ph.D. thesis*.

Glaser B, Strauss A (1967) *The Discovery of Grounded Theory* (Weidenfield & Nicolson, London, UK).

González-Díaz J, Sánchez-Rodríguez E (2007) A natural selection from the core of a TU game: The core-center. *International Journal of Game Theory* 36(1):27-46.

Granot D, Sošić G (2005) Formation of alliances in internet-based supply exchanges. *Management Science* 51(1):92-105.

Gul F (1989) Bargaining foundations of Shapley value. *Econometrica: Journal of the Econometric Society* 57(1):81-95.

Hart S, Kurz M (1983) Endogenous formation of coalitions. *Econometrica: Journal of the Econometric Society*:1047-1064.

Heller MA, Eisenberg RS (1998) Can patents deter innovation? The anticommons in biomedical research. *Science* 280(5364):698-701.

Henderson RM, Clark KB (1990) Architectural innovation: The reconfiguration of existing product technologies and the failure of established firms. *Administrative Science Quarterly* 35(1):9-30.

Hendrikse G (2011) Pooling, access, and countervailing power in channel governance. *Management Science* 67(9):1692-1702.

Henkel J, Baldwin C, Shih W (2013) IP modularity: Profiting from innovation by aligning product architecture with intellectual property. *California Management Review* 55(4):65-82.

Henkel J, Hoffmann A (2014) Value capture in hierarchically organized industries: The hierarchy strategy. *Working paper*, http://geaba.de/pdf/2014Henkel.pdf.

Hoetker G (2006) Do modular products lead to modular organizations? *Strategic Management Journal* 27(6):501-518.

Iansiti M, Levien R (2004) *The Keystone Advantage: What the New Dynamics of Business Ecosystems mean for Strategy, Innovation, and Sustainability* (Harvard Business School Press, Boston, MA).

Inderst R, Wey C (2001) Bargaining, mergers and technology choice in bilaterally oligopolistic industries. *CEPR Discussion Paper No. 2981*, http://ssrn.com/abstract=287607.

Jacobides MG, Knudsen T, Augier M (2006) Benefiting from innovation: Value creation, value appropriation and the role of industry architectures. *Research Policy* 35(8):1200-1221.

Jacobides MG, MacDuffie JP (2013) How to drive value your way. *Harvard Business Review* 91(7):92-100.

Kattuman PA, Rodriguez D, Sharapov D, Velazquez FJ (2011) Revisiting Profitability: Firm, Business Group, Industry and Country Effects. *Academy of Management Proceedings* 1:1-6.

Kotha S, Nolan R, Condit PM (2005) *Boeing 787: The Dreamliner, Case 305-101* (Harvard Business School, Boston, MA).

Kotha S, Srikanth K (2013) Managing a global partnership model: Lessons from the Boeing 787 'Dreamliner'program. *Global Strategy Journal* 3(1):41-66.

Krauss RM (1966) Structural and attitudinal factors in interpersonal bargaining. *Journal of Experimental Social Psychology* 2(1):42-55.

Kreps D (1990) *Game Theory and Economic Modelling* (Oxford University Press, Oxford, UK).

Lamnek S (1995) *Qualitative Sozialforschung, Band 1: Methodologie*, Vol.3 (Psychologie Verlags Union, Weinheim, Germany).

Langlois RN (2003) The vanishing hand: The changing dynamics of industrial capitalism. *Industrial and Corporate Change* 12(2):351-385.

Langlois RN, Garzarelli G (2008) Of hackers and hairdressers: Modularity and the organizational economics of open-source collaboration. *Industry and Innovation* 15(2):125-143.

Langlois RN, Robertson PL (1992) Networks and innovation in a modular system: Lessons from the microcomputer and stereo component industries. *Research Policy* 21:297-313.

Layne-Farrar A, Padilla AJ, Schmalensee R (2007) Pricing patents for licensing in standard-setting organizations: Making sense of FRAND commitments. *Antitrust Law Journal* 74(3):671-706.

Lee HL, Sasser MM (1995) Product universality and design. *Production Planning and Control* 6(3):270-277.

Lemley MA, Shapiro C (2007) Patent holdup and royalty stacking. *Texas Law Review* 85:1991-2049.

Lepak DP, Smith KG, Taylor MS (2007) Value creation and value capture: A multilevel perspective. *Academy of Management Review* 32(1):180-194.

Lerner J, Tirole J (2002) Some simple economics of open source. *The Journal of Industrial Economics* 50(2):197-234.

Lippman SA, Rumelt RP (2003) A bargaining perspective on resource advantage. *Strategic Management Journal* 24(11):1069-1086.

Luo J, Baldwin CY, Whitney DE, Magee CL (2012) The architecture of transaction networks: A comparative analysis of hierarchy in two sectors. *Industrial and Corporate Change* 21(6):1307-1335.

MacDonald G, Ryall MD (2004) How do value creation and competition determine whether a firm appropriates value? *Management Science* 50(10):1319-1333.

MacDuffie JP, Helper S (2007) Collaboration in supply chains: With and without trust. Heckscher C, Adler P, eds. *The Firm as a Collaborative Community* (Oxford University Press, New York, NY).

Michener HA, Dettman DC, Richardson GD, Julseth DC (1987) A test of the characteristic function and the Harsanyi function in N-person normal form sidepayment games. *Theory and decision* 23(2):161-187.

Michener HA, Ginsberg IJ, Yuen K (1979) Effects of core properties in four-person games with side-payments. *Behavioral Science* 24(4):263-280.

Michener H.A., Potter K., Sakurai M.M. (1983) On the predictive efficiency of the core solution in side-payment games. *Theory and Decision* 15(1):11-28.

Michener HA, Potter K, Sakurai MM (1983) On the predictive efficiency of the core solution in side-payment games. *Theory and Decision* 15(1):11-28.

Moene KO, Wallerstein M, Hoel M (1993) Bargaining structure and economic performance. Flanagan RJ, Moene KO, Wallerstein M *Trade Union Behaviour, Pay-Bargaining, and Economic Performance* (Oxford University Press, Oxford. UK).

Morris CR, Ferguson CH (1993) How architecture wins technology wars. *Harvard Business Review* 71(2):86-96.

Murnighan JK, Roth AE (1977) The effects of communication and information availability in an experimental study of a three-person game. *Management Science* 23(12):1336-1348.

Myerson RB (1977) Graphs and cooperation in games. *Mathematics of Operations Research* 2(3):225-229.

Nagarajan M, Sošić G (2008) Game-theoretic analysis of cooperation among supply chain agents: Review and extensions. *European Journal of Operational Research* 187(3):719-745.

Open Source Initiative (2014) *The Open Source Definition*. Last accessed 15 Jan 2014, http://opensource.org/osd.

Open Source Initiative (2014) *The open source definition*. Last accessed 15 Jan 2014, http://opensource.org/osd.

Owen G (1977) Values of Games with a priori Unions. Henn R, Moeschlin O, eds. *Essays in Mathematical Economics & Game Theory* (Springer, Berlin, Germany).

Pérez-Castrillo D, Wettstein D (2001) Bidding for the surplus: A non-cooperative approach to the Shapley value. *Journal of Economic Theory* 100(2):274-294.

Pisano GP, Teece DJ (2007) How to capture value from innovation: Shaping intellectual property and industry architecture. *California Management Review* 50(1):278-296.

Porter ME (1980) *Competitive Strategy: Techniques for Analyzing Industries and Competitors* (Free Press, New York, NY).

Pritchard D, MacPherson A (2004) Industrial subsidies and the politics of world trade: The case of the Boeing 7e7. *Industrial Geographer* 1(2):57-73.

Pulido MA, Sánchez-Soriano J (2009) On the core, the Weber set and convexity in games with a priori unions. *European Journal of Operational Research* 193(2):468-475.

Quies P (2012) Valuing standard essential patents. An examination of announced FRAND royalty rates for LTE. *Whitepaper, Micronomics Inc*, http://www.americanbar.org/content/dam/aba/publications/litigation_committees/intellectual/012413-valuing-standard-essential-patents-memo.authcheckdam.pdf.

Raymond ES (1999) *The Cathedral and the Bazaar: Musings on Linux and Open Source by an Accidental Revolutionary* (O'Reilly Media, Sebastopol, CA).

Ro Y, Fixson SK, Liker JK (2008) Modularity and supplier involvement in product development. Loch C, Kavadias S, eds. *Handbook of New Product Development Management* (Butterworth-Heinemann, Burlington, MA, USA).

Rumelt RP (1984) Towards a strategic theory of the firm. Lamb R *Competitive Strategic Management* (Prentice Hall, Englewood Cliffs, NJ).

Ryall MD, Sorenson O (2007) Brokers and competitive advantage. *Management Science* 53(4):566-583.

Sanchez R, Mahoney JT (1996) Modularity, flexibility, and knowledge management in product and organization design. *Strategic Management Journal* 17:63-76.

Santos FM, Eisenhardt KM (2009) Constructing markets and shaping boundaries: Entrepreneurial power in nascent fields. *Academy of Management Journal* 52(4):643-671.

Shapiro C (2001) Navigating the patent thicket: Cross licenses, patent pools, and standard setting. Jaffe AB, Lerner J, Stern S, eds. *Innovation Policy and the Economy*, Vol.1 (MIT Press, Boston).

Shapley L.S. (1952) *Notes on the n-Person Game, III: Some Variants of the von Neumann-Morgenstern Definition of Solution. RM-670* (The RAND Corporation, Santa Monica, CA).

Shapley L.S. (1953) A value for n-Person Games. Kuhn A.W., Tucker A.W., eds. *Contributions to the Theory of Games Vol II* (Princeton University Press, Princeton).

Shapley LS (1953) A value for n-Person Games. Kuhn AW, Tucker AW, eds. *Contributions to the Theory of Games Vol II* (Princeton University Press, Princeton NJ).

Shapley L.S. (1971) Cores of convex games. *International Journal of Game Theory* 1(1):11-26.

Shih W (2014) *Boeing 787 Manufacturing Footprint, Case N9-614-049* (Harvard Business School, Boston, MA).

Shih W, Pierson M (2012) *Modularity in Design and Manufacturing: Application to Commercial Aircraft, Case 9-612-035* (Harvard Business School, Boston, MA).

Simchi-Levi D, Kaminsky P, Simchi-Levi E (2008) *Designing and Managing the Supply Chain: Concepts, Strategies, and Case Studies* (McGraw-Hil/Irwin, New York, NY).

Simon HA (1962) The architecture of complexity. *Proceedings of the American Philosophical Society* 106(6):467-482.

Strauss A, Corbin JM (1990) *Basics of Qualitative Research: Grounded Theory Procedures and Techniques* (SAGE Publications, Thousand Oaks, CA).

Sturgeon TJ (2001) How do we define value chains and production networks? *IDS Bulletin* 32(3):9-18.

Sturgeon TJ (2002) Modular production networks: A new American model of industrial organization. *Industrial and Corporate Change* 11(3):451-496.

Tang CS, Zimmerman JD (2010) Managing new product development and supply chain risks: The Boeing 787 case. *Supply Chain Forum: An International Journal* 10(2):74-86.

Teece DJ (1986) Profiting from technological innovation: Implications for integration, collaboration, licensing and public policy. *Research Policy* 15(6):285-305.

Thomas L, Autio E, Gann D (2014) Architectural leverage: Putting platforms in context. *The Academy of Management Perspectives* 28(2):198-219.

Williamson OE (1985) *The Economic Institutions of Capitalism: Firms, Markets, Relational Contracting* (Free Press, New York, NY).

Williamson OE (1991) Comparative economic organization: The analysis of discrete structural alternatives. *Administrative Science Quarterly* 36(2):269-296.

Winter E. (2002) The Shapley value. *Handbook of Game Theory with Wconomic Applications*:2025-2054.

Yin RK (1984) *Case Study Research*, Vol.1 (SAGE Publications, Thousand Oaks, CA).

Ziedonis RH (2004) Don't fence me in: Fragmented markets for technology and the patent acquisition strategies of firms. *Management Science* 50(6):804-820.

Zirpoli F, Camuffo A (2009) Product architecture, inter-firm vertical coordination and knowledge partitioning in the auto industry. *European Management Review* 6(4):250-264.

MIX
Papier aus verantwortungsvollen Quellen
Paper from responsible sources
FSC® C105338

If you have any concerns about our products,
you can contact us on
ProductSafety@springernature.com

In case Publisher is established outside the EU,
the EU authorized representative is:
Springer Nature Customer Service Center GmbH
Europaplatz 3, 69115 Heidelberg, Germany

Printed by Libri Plureos GmbH
in Hamburg, Germany